Coder Cole: Python

An Introduction to Programming

By Cole Hersowitz

ISBN: 1544150229

ISBN-13: 978-1544150222

codercole.com

DEDICATION

I would like to dedicate this book to my friends, parents, peers, and teachers. I would also like to recognize my mentors and my cousin Dale Hersowitz who helped spark my interest in technology.

CONTENTS

ACKNOWLEDGMENTS

I would like to thank Mr. Marquez Garrett, a teacher at my school, for listening to my ideas and helping me with a portion of this project. I would also like to recognize all friends and family members who have helped support me with my endeavors.

About the Author

While there is a large push to get more kids involved in computer science, much of this movement is being led by government officials and industry leaders. This book is actually written by a kid who learned to code by self-studying the subject, and he wants to share his knowledge with others. After attending a summer program at Stanford University to learn basic Java programming as an incoming middle school student, Cole taught himself iOS development and launched his first game to the app store. Pelican Plunge, a 2-D adventure developed with the Corona SDK, was downloaded in twenty-four countries within a single day of its release.

Shortly after this experience, Cole became interested in mobile marketing and developed an application called Yep Promos. This new application sent local notifications containing targeted promotions to users within one hundred meters of a Yep registered business. Cole offered this geo-fencing technology to local businesses in Orange County, California. With an interest in technology and business, Cole has held summer internships at startup companies in Irvine. Understanding the importance of community service, he has also founded the YEP for Kids Foundation, a 501-(c)(3) nonprofit organization that runs after school coding classes. The organization is trying to expand their computer science education model by establishing YEP for Kids clubs at high schools that serve as volunteer bases for surrounding coding classes.

Cole is currently a junior at Corona del Mar High School in Newport Beach, California. Most recently, he has been taking computer science courses at University of California Irvine. He has experience with Python, Swift, AngularJS, HTML5, Java, and some PHP. As a kid who learned to code, Cole knows what it takes to progress through the learning curve. Cole noticed students at his high school struggling with the course work of the newly-added AP Computer Science A class. He knew he could do something to help his peers considering he faced the same obstacles as a young person learning to code. Cole strongly believes kids should be writing actual programs instead of using browser programs or drag-and-drop languages. Instead of learning to problem solve and debug, these programs don't always enable kids to develop a true understanding of the material. He also thinks these programs create a false perception of computer programming. The minute his peers try to move towards a more advanced coding goal such as building a mobile app, they often give up. This book is the introduction Cole would've liked to have when he first started coding.

Introduction Rant

Today, technology is business, whether you like it or not. Software is a predominant part of almost every industry sector including finance, medicine, agriculture, and manufacturing. On a daily basis, people are impacted by the execution of millions of lines codes that were developed by programmers to make iOS applications, websites, motor control systems, smart thermostats, and cars. Facebook's website has over 50 million lines of code while an average modern car such as a Ford has upwards of 100 million lines. In this information age, the rise of cloud computing, smart phones, automation, 3D printing, and other technologies is spurring a digital revolution. Automation has the potential to displace workers by replacing humans that perform repetitive tasks a machine is capable of. According to a 2013 study conducted by Carl Benedikt Frey and Michael A. Osborne from the Oxford Martin School, an estimated 47 percent of total US employment is susceptible to computerization, specifically those working in transportation and logistics occupations.

Although software may replace some jobs in particular sectors such as manufacturing, it is also creating new software engineering jobs. According to code.org, there are more than 500,000 unfilled computing jobs and programming jobs are the number one source of new wages. Coding truly has evolved into the new literacy of the Augmented Age.

Even if you don't become a software engineer or work in a computing job, you will still be impacted by its prominence in industry. Developing at least a fundamental understanding of programming is a valuable skillset for future employment opportunities and understanding the implications of technology use. Although technology can be beneficial to humanity, some uncontrolled future developments such as artificial super intelligence can potentially harm society, and it's important that citizens of this world are informed decision makers when directing technological innovation. For example, the Internet of Things is a concept in which most every object is connected to the web including your refrigerator, house appliances, milk carton, shoes - just about anything. Although this science-fiction like network will automatically order new milk when it's running low, make toast in the morning, or turn on the thermostat five minutes before you will arrive home, its potential implications including privacy limitations and security vulnerabilities must be considered. Technology is such an integral part of this generation that it's rather naïve to not have some understanding of how it works and the software that controls billions of devices.

The disruption is coming much sooner than most people expect. We must not resist these changes as luddites once did, but we must adapt and embrace the innovation. Welcoming technological changes does not come free of contingencies as we must respect the rights of individuals, respect privacy, respect security, and ensure that innovations thrust humanity forward instead of becoming a subtle threat. UPS is currently in the process of testing a delivery system in which drones are released from trucks along a route to deliver a package and they return to the truck at its new location along the route. Amazon has been testing their Prime Air system which will be able to deliver packages to customers in 30 minutes or less. As government regulation begins to embrace new technologies, drone delivery will exit its testing phase and become available for consumers. The problem is government doesn't always understand the possible implications of new technology and how to appropriately regulate it. One of the most recent controversies surrounds the security vulnerabilities of smart TVs - a device located in approximately 46% of households according to the Consumer Technology Association. Security experts claim it is only a matter of time before black hat hackers will exploit these systems through apps and programs on these TVs that contain security vulnerabilities. Smart TV manufacturers are aware of some of the vulnerabilities, yet they are only now trying to address the risks.

The rate of innovation may deviate from the mean but it isn't likely to be significantly lower anytime in the near future. In 1965, Gordon Moore, the cofounder of Intel, summarized the rate at which the power of computer chips improve in a law that became known as Moore's Law. This law states that technological innovation grows exponentially over time, and Moore's original claim was that the count of components in integrated chips would double every eighteen months. A 2013 study conducted by MIT and Santa Fe Institutes suggests that Moore's law is still a reasonable approximation of technological innovation over short time spans. As growth in hardware and software are likely to continue booming, society is going to become even more connected to technology. This innovation will add conveniences, but will also add difficulties, ethical considerations, and cultural changes.

This book is designed to teach you the basics of coding in the Python programming language so that you are code literate, and you can apply the learned concepts to other applications or languages. As an introduction, this book covers the constructs that are shared across almost all languages, although some are Python specific. By the end of this book, I can't promise that you will be able to build the next Facebook or build an artificially intelligent system like Mark Zuckerberg's project, Jarvis, but you will have the tools you need to learn more about an area of interest such as game development and pursue a project. If you plan on enrolling in AP Computer Science A at school or self-challenging the AP test, this book doesn't cover Java, but the concepts acquired will still be helpful to develop a fundamental understanding of the material. This book may be specifically helpful in developing your coding skills if you plan on taking AP Computer Science Principles.

The one thing I ask in this process is that you be persistent. My friend once told me that learning to code is not a sprint - it's a marathon. You may at first be excited but then quickly become frustrated when your code doesn't run or you don't understand a concept, but be persistent. A concept will become clearer over time and it's such a rewarding experience to conquer a programming problem. During the learning process, carefully read the code examples that are presented. Try to understand each line of code, why it was written, and how it could possibly be restructured. When working on coding exercises, make sure you know why you are writing a line of code and be sure to frequently comment your code (a practice we will discuss later). My friend and I were helping elementary school students with a basic Python problem set. A student was really struggling to get their code working, and my friend told them "If you don't know what you want to do, how is the computer supposed to know?"

Programming is about problem solving and troubleshooting. Computers are innately moronic. It takes the cognitive effort of a human to get them to perform a task. Before solving a problem or building an application, it's essential you understand the underlying process and can explain it before writing code. Why do you think programmers and trendy tech startups like whiteboards and glass windows so much?

Python (not the snake)

You picked up this book and saw it has the word "Python" on the cover. That has nothing to do with the type of snake. Created in the 1990s as a successor to the language ABC by Guido van Rossum in the Netherlands, This book is about the programming language Python. It is open source and maintained by the Python Software Foundation , a 501(c)(3) non-profit corporation that holds the intellectual property rights behind the language. Python is utilized within large applications and organizations including Yahoo, IBM, Battlefield 2, NASA, and the Central Intelligence Agency. Its popularity extends into science, research, and it even runs on the low-cost computers created by the Raspberry Pi Foundation. College courses including Stanford's CS41, MIT's Introduction to Computer Science, and UC Berkeley's COMPSCI 9H use Python as their language of choice for introducing computer science.

One of the reasons Python is used to introduce programming is that it's versatile and it syntactically tends to be more human readable, thus less cryptic, than some other languages. For example, even if you've never coded before, look at the block of code below and try to predict what the program will do when run.

```
daylight = True


if daylight == False:
    print("turn on the street lights")
else:
     print("turn off the lights, it's bright")
```

It's okay if this code looks slightly intimidating, but it's actually very straightforward once you learn the basics of programming. Since daylight is a variable that is set to True, the statement "turn of the lights, it's bright out" will be printed to the console since the first condition wasn't met. Even though you may have never seen code before, you could have correctly guessed what the program will do. That's why we are using Python - it allows us to focus on programming concepts and problem solving rather than the intricacies of typing in a more cryptic-looking language like C++ or Java.

Python Install

Alright, let's initiate the learning process and start writing some Python code. The first step is to install Python on your computer. For this book, I encourage you to download some version of Python 3 (download link: https://www.Python.org/downloads/) because some of the code in this book will be different than the conventions used for Python 2.7. After downloading Python, double click on the download and follow the install instructions that are prompted on the screen.

Once the install is complete, search for a program called IDLE, the default Python development environment that is included with the Python install. A shell is a computer window that takes bash commands to perform operations on a computer such as changing directories, removing a file, or checking your IP address. To verify that Python has been properly installed, open an application called Terminal if you are on a Mac or Command Prompt if you are using Windows. Throughout this book, I will be using a Mac so if I reference Terminal and you are using a different operating system, use the corresponding shell program.

Once the shell has opened, type “Python” and verify that it has started running by looking for three carrots (>>>) that should appear on a subsequent line.

Hello World

It's time to write your first Python program, Hello World. It's the first example in nearly every new language a programmer learns and it was created by Brian Kernighan in his 1978 book, C Programming Language. We are now going to transition to the application called IDLE that was previously mentioned. Open IDLE, you should notice a Python shell that is denoted with three carrots.

Type the following code and press return on your keyboard:

```
print("Hello World")
```

Immediately, the words "Hello World" were output in the shell on the line below. Congratulations, you've just written your first Python program! As minute as this program is, it's a giant step on your journey to learn Python.

Commenting

Comments are notes programmers add in code that are not executed by the interpreter to describe how a program is setup, leave a reminder, or any sort of helpful information. They are extremely important because after writing thousands of lines of code, programmers often forget how the code they wrote earlier works and sometimes are better off scrapping a project and re-writing the code than working with messy, uncommented code. Besides leaving helpful reminders, comments are an essential part of team collaboration so that others can read your code, understand how it's supposed to function, and help debug it. Even though someone writes code and it may just barely function, that isn't good enough. It is essential you write clean, minimalistic code that is frequently commented. With small programs, commenting may seem pointless at times, but I highly encourage you to do it anyways.

Comments are ignored when your code is executed so you can write virtually anything – sentences, emojis, Chinese – whatever is helpful. There are two main classifications of comments: single line comments and multiline comments.

Single line comments are denoted with a hash sign. You can have a single line comment after a line of code, on the line above, or on the line below. They are useful for briefly describing a function, variable, or expression.

```
# this is a single line comment above
# ignored by Python interpreter
print("Hello World")     # outputs hello world
# above were some comment placement examples
```

Multiline comments are denoted with three single quotations. It's important that you open a multiline comment with three single quotations, and close it with three single quotations at the end of your comments. These comments are better for leaving longer notes in a program. Generally, these longer comments are used to describe the basic contents of a file or a setup – something that can't easily be described in a single line.

```
''' This is an example of a multi-line comment.
You could write whatever you want to
   Inside the quotes. Just make sure you close
the comment '''
print("Hello World")
```

Semi-colons

In a plethora of other languages including Java and C++, lines of code normally must end with a semicolon. In Python, we do not need to use them. If you add one after a function call or variable declaration, the Python program will still run, but it is completely unnecessary.

Batch Mode vs. Interactive

In our first hello world program, we were using Python interactively. An interactive session is when a program is dependent on a user typing commands that are immediately executed. That's exactly what we did with hello world. We called the print function, entered a message, and after pressing return it was immediately output in the console. The issue with interactive sessions is that they are dependent on user input and we cannot edit the code we wrote earlier in the shell nor can we save it. Going forward, we will be using batch processing so that we can save our code and execute several commands at once. Batch processing occurs when we write our code in a file and then run it after saving the file. This is how we practically develop large programs, save our code, and collaborate with other programmers.

Let's take our hello world program and use batch process instead. In IDLE, click File -> New File. Then, on the first line add a single line comment. On the next line, print *hello world* to the screen (see the code below).

```
# Hello world program in a Python file
print("Hello World")
```

After writing the print statement above, click File -> Save. Give your file a name such as *hello.py* and be sure it has the *.py* extension. After saving, click Run -> Run Module. The code you wrote in the file will then be executed in a Python shell. Your code is now editable, meaning you can change “Hello World” to “Hello USA”, save it, and re-run the program if you’d like to. It’s important that when you save a Python code file, you must save it with the *.py* extension for it to work. It can’t be a *.txt* file, *.csv* file, or any other type.

Important Note About Examples

Due to limitations with the size of book pages, some code statements in the examples throughout this book are shown on two lines when they should really be written on the same line. If the content between an open parenthesis and close parenthesis is not on the same line in an example due to the length of the statement, write it on the same line in your actual code file.

Debrief

Okay, hopefully you’ve got Python running and could complete the hello world program. In the first chapter, we are going to be discussing our first major concept: variables. This *Hello World* program is quite simple, but it is a classic starter to the power of programing. The applications used by people daily are composed of layers of different software components that complete the app ranging from handling networking to the graphical user interface to local storage.

After writing Python programs, you will likely develop a new appreciation for the applications, websites, and other programs you use daily. The development of remarkable applications such as Facebook, Slack, and Snapchat is no small task. It's a large collaborative effort between teams of engineers, managers, QA testers, and others, not the result of a mythical genius programmer. Software development is fundamentally about social collaboration, problem solving, efficiency, and persistence.

Ch. 1 Variables in Python

Data Types and Variables

A variable is a programming construct that represents data such as a number or a word that can be modified or used later. In math, you've encountered variables in courses such as Algebra I where *x* represents a value and can be plugged into an algebraic equation. There are different forms of data we encounter in the world such as sentences composed of multiple words, decimal numbers that represent temperature, whole numbers that represent shirt sizes, and binary conditions such as whether it's day or night. All these scenarios contain different data types or classifications of data.

Variables are essential to any decent size program to keep track of user input, data that is being processed, program features, and a plethora of other factors. For example, in many games like Angry Birds, there is a variable that represents the player's score and changes its value according to whether the player gains points or not. In applications that require an account login, the username and password entered by the user are often stored in variables. These are vital constructs to any programming language and software development project. Trying to code without them would be like trying to ride a bike without wheels, an utter waste of time.

Variable Input Exercise

Let's try writing a small program that uses a variable to take the user's name and greet them in the Python console. Create a new Python file (Click file -> New File in IDLE), then save it as *input_exercise.py*. Add the following code:

```
# take input from the user and print welcome
#message
name = input("What is your name? ")
print("Welcome " + name)
```

Run the program (Run -> Run Module) and notice how it prompts you to enter input. Enter your name and press return. Notice how the welcome message is printed in the console.

```
What is your name? Cole
Welcome, Cole
```

This code uses the built-in Python input function to prompt the user to enter a value. After they enter their name, this value is assumed in place of the variable in the print statement on the following line. Without the use of variables, we wouldn't be able to take user input because we would have to hard code a name in the print statement or we would need to call the input function inside the print statement which would be messy.

Data Types

To represent the various types of data, it's important you fully understand data types which is the way data is classified in programming. Not all objects are created equal. The classification of data types is like the states of matter: each has its own qualities and properties such as the way a liquid can change shape to fit the container it's in but a solid retains the same shape. Here are the main data types you should be aware of:

String: represents words or a series of characters. Encapsulated within a set of double or single quotations. Examples: a sentence is a string, jar, word, 4534%$@%

```
# various variable declarations of type String
message = “A message is considered a string”
name = “John Doe”
area = “32” # string since it’s in quotes
secret_code = “%%$5&*(&((”
```

Integer: represents a whole number, can be either negative or positive. Examples: 5, -43563, 25466, 1, 0, 12

```
# various variables that are Integers
# Notice there are no quotations
# Quotes around a number make it a string
student_count = 31
building_number = 244
num = 10
```

Float: represents a decimal number, can also be either negative or positive. Examples: 3.14, 22.0, 2.3333333

```
# various variables that are Floats
percentage_complete = 89.53
temperature = 72.0  # still considered a float
since it's written with a decimal
example = 657.3432445423
```

Boolean: represents a condition, only assumes two values: True or False. In assigning a Boolean value, the first letters of the words true and false must be capitalized.

```
# various variables that are Boolean values
working = True
```

```
passed test = False
lights_on = True
```

Variables in Python are dynamic, meaning they can change data types. While this can be advantageous, there are also drawbacks that could cause your programs to perform an unintended action. For example, you may make a variable an integer, but then try to print it to the screen as a string, thus causing your program to crash. The dynamic typing in Python is very different from other languages such as Java where you must set the type when declaring the variable and it cannot be changed in what is known as static typing. For example, if you create an integer in Java called score and decide you want to make it into a float point value, you cannot simply assign your old variable a decimal value. Instead, you must create an entirely new variable to store this value.

Declaring Variables

Initializing a variable in Python is very simple: you choose the name of your variable and assign it a value with an equals sign. Unlike other languages, you do not need to declare the variable data type before the name. See the structure below for the syntax.

```
# the variable is named var
```

```
# the data can be any type or object
var = data goes here
```

You can give your variable any name, except you can't use Python reserved words such as *in*, *as*, and *assert*. It's important to name your variable something relevant to the data it will contain so that your code is more readable in the future. For multiword variable names, camel casing is the standard naming convention in languages such as Java, but in Python the convention is to separate words with an underscore. To be aware of it for other programming languages, camel casing is a naming convention for compound names in which the first letter of the first word isn't capitalized, but the first letter of subsequent words are. For example, userData or eventStartTime would both follow proper camel casing conventions. For the variable naming convention in Python, see the structure below:

```
my_variable_name = data goes here
```

String Operations

Strings can be manipulated with several Python functions available to us. An important operation in programming is concatenation – the action of combining strings together. The plus sign is used for concatenation and you can combine two or more strings. For example, the code below combines a string and a variable of type string to print out a full statement.

```
to_destination = “Orange County”
from_destination = “New York”
print(“The plane landed in “ + to_destination +
“ after flying from ” + from_destination)
```

The code above would output the following after concatenating the strings:

```
>>> The plane landed in Orange County after
flying from New York
```

A common scenario when programming is to check two strings to see if they are equal. We check for string equality using two equals signs, which will return a Boolean value depending on if the compared strings are exactly the same. The comparison is case sensitive and spaces do count. For example:

```
“Mikey” == “Mikey”    # returns true since they
#are exactly the same
“mikey” == “Mikey”    # returns false since the
#first m is lowercase
```

```
" Mikey" == "Mikey"   # returns false since
#there is a space in the first string
```

Sometimes, to make string comparisons easy, we want to make a string either all uppercase or all lowercase. For example, if you ask a user to enter a color and you want to use if statements to check if the color they entered equals red or green, you should convert the input to all uppercase or lowercase and compare it to the corresponding capitalization. This is important because if the program checks for the input "red," but the user enters "reD", the expression will return false. As a result, the contents within the if statement will not be executed since the string values are not equal. The lower and upper functions are available for us to convert to a capitalization standard. See the example below for syntax.

```
company1 = "Acorns"
print(company1.upper())    # notice the upper
#function is called with its name
print(company1.lower())    # two parenthesis are
#used to call the function

company2 = "SouthWEST"
```

```
print(company2.upper())# output - SOUTHWESTs
print(company2.lower())  # output - southwest
```

The previous example would output the following in the Python console:

```
>>> ACORNS
>>> acorns
>>> SOUTHWEST
>>> southwest
```

Float and Integer Operations

Similar to how we can perform mathematical operations to numbers, we can do the same thing in Python. Here is a table of the operations:

Symbol	Operation	Notes
a + b	addition	Add a to b
a - b	subtraction	Subtract b from a
a * b	multiplication	Multiply a by b
a % b	modulo	The remainder of a divided by b
a**b	exponential	Base a raised to the b power

These operations generally follow PEMDAS like in math class for the order of operations (Parenthesis, Exponents, Multiplication, Division, Addition, Subtraction). If you are unsure of the order in which an expression will be evaluated, use parenthesis in the expression to make sure you get the intended outcome. Using parenthesis, even if the operations are in the correct order, is a good practice so that you can immediately figure out how the expression is evaluated without having to recall the order of operations.

```
n1 = 2 + 4 - 9 + 1  # value is -2
n2 = (3*5) / 2  # value is 7.5
n3 = 8 % 3  # value is 2 because the remainder
of 8/3 is 2
n4 = 2**3  # value is 8
```

Casting

Sometimes in programming, you need to use casting to convert a variable from one data type to another. For example, you may need to convert a string to an integer so that you can perform mathematical operations on it. You will often find that you need to print a statement and some quantitative value such as an integer, but you can't pass an integer into the print function without casting it into a string. A common scenario for casting occurs when you use the input function to collect a number the user wants to enter, but the input function returns a string so you must convert it to an integer or float. Reference the next example.

```
degrees_farenheight = input("What is the
temperature in fahrenheit? ") # string value
result = (float(degrees_farenheight) * 32) -
(5/9)  # cast to float so we can perform math
print(str(result) + " degrees celsius") # cast
# result to string so it can be printed
```

The following would happen when the program is run:

```
What is the temperature in fahrenheit? 72.5
22.5 degrees celsius
>>>
```

The subsequent table contains function calls to cast from one data type to another. Each function takes a variable or data as input, what we call an argument in Python (sometimes called parameters in other languages). Note that the argument you would like to cast must contain the appropriate value or you will receive a value error. For example, the string "73" can be casted to an integer (73) or a float (73.0), but the string "$" cannot be casted to either of these types due to the value of the string. The "$" symbol cannot be quantified as an integer or float.

Function	Description
str(*argument*)	Converts data to a string
int(*argument*)	Converts data to an integer
float(*argument*)	Converts data to a decimal value
bool(*argument*)	Converts data to a boolean

The code below is an example of how values would change when casted:

```
num = 72 # originally an integer
num = str(num) # now a string so it’s
#equivalent to num = “72”
num = float(num) # now a decimal number, 72.0
num = bool(num) # not 0 so it returns true
```

Lists

A list, sometimes called an array in other languages, is a data structure that allows us to hold other lists, variables, objects, or data values. Lists are useful because they can hold a series of data such as the last ten test scores for a student. Another potential use for a list is setting one up that contains all the users who liked a post on Instagram to output this result to the account owner. Lists can contain data of any type, meaning you could have a list of multiple float values, integer values, or a mix of other values. A list is initialized with square brackets, and data can optionally be passed in upon the list's creation or the list can be left empty. Items, the elements of a list, are separated with a comma, like how you would separate items on a to-do list with a bullet point or dash. See the example below for syntax.

```
followers = [“johnnyboy1”, “lmartin”, “jmoney”,
“ctabor”]  # initialize a list with followers
first_follower = followers[0]  # assumes the
#value “johnnyboy1”, the first list item
likes = [] # initialized an empty list
```

As demonstrated above, we can access an item in a list by referencing its index. In Python, the indices start at zero, meaning there is one less index than the length of the list (n - 1 in which n = list length). For example, the last index of a list containing 12 items is 11. If you tried to reference a 12th index in the list, this would cause an *IndexError* and the program would crash if this error wasn't accounted for. Although positive indices are used more frequently, items in a list can also be accessed with a negative index that is in the range of negative one and the list length (from -1 to -n). A negative index references items from the end of the list rather than the beginning. When someone refers to the length of the list, they are describing the number of elements in that list, not the highest index number. The table below shows the indices for our followers list we initialized in the last example which has a length of four:

0	1	2	3
johnnyboy1	lmartin	jmoney	ellieya
-4	-3	-2	-1

Here are more examples of valid lists that contain various data types:

```
depths = [23.4, 36.74, 99.999, 150.32, 146.723,
19.01]  # example lists of ocean depths
#containing floats
print(depths[-2]) # outputs 146.723

junk = ["swagger", 54.40, "$$", 23, 0]  # lists
#can contain different data types; they don't
#all have to be the same
print(junk[0]) # outputs 'swagger'
```

After initializing a list, you may need to add data, delete it, update it, or perform another operation without creating a new list.

Here are some useful methods that can be called on lists. In the table, the list is hypothetically named *list* but this value would be substituted for the actual variable that contains the list.

function	description
list.append(*x*)	Adds item *x* to the list
list.insert(*i, x*)	*i* is the index you would like to insert the item at, *x* is the item
list.clear()	Removes all items in a list
del list[*i*]	Delete an item in a list at index *i*
list.count(*x*)	Returns the number of times item *x* appears in a list
len(list)	Returns the length of the list

The next set of examples demonstrates how the functions above would modify a list. Notice how the *insert* function overrides the value already existent at the index passed into the function.

```
following = ["jj_shay", "tcruz1", "the_donald", "kkramer"]
```

```
following.append(“jbrown”)  # following would
#yield the items above and jbrown at the end

following.insert(0, “jumpman”)  # jj_shay would
# be replaced with “jumpman”
del following[0]  # deletes “jumpman” (the 0
#element) from the list
following.count(“the_donald”)  # returns 1
#because “the_donald” only appears once
len(following)  # returns 4, the number of
#items in the list
```

Often, programmers need to store data in multidimensional lists (lists that contain other lists instead of integers or another data type). We access an element in a multidimensional list by first indexing the outer lists for a list item and then indexing that item. For example, let’s say we want to initialize a list that contains lists of x and y coordinates.

```
points = [[0, 22], [3, 5], [5, 9]]
points[0][0]  # value is 0 - the zeroth element
#of the first list item
points[1][0]  # value is 3 - the zeroth element
#of the second item
```

```
Points[2][1]  # value is 9 - the first element
#of the third item
```

In the example above, the *points* list is two dimensional because it is a list containing lists. There are no limits on the depth of a list as long as your computer doesn't run out of memory. This means a multidimensional list could be three dimensional (list containing lists containing lists), four dimensional, or deeper. A two-dimensional list is the most practical multidimensional list because any further depth can make the list unwieldy to use.

Dictionaries

Sometimes, we want the ability to store multiple items in a data structure, but we do not want to worry about the index of which we are accessing the element, such as the case when using a list. The items can be unsorted, but we need some means of accessing them. Luckily, we have dictionaries – data structures that enable us to store key value pairs. The data inside a dictionary is unordered, and we can initialize one with a set of curly braces. The next example contains the syntax for a dictionary.

```
name_here = {"key1": "value1", "key2":
"value2", "key3": "value3" }  # can initialize
#with just { } for an empty dictionary
```

Generally, the keys of a dictionary are strings and they can be denoted with either single or double quotations. To access a value in a dictionary, we simply reference the key using square brackets. We can also delete a key-value pair in a dictionary and return a list of all the keys existent. To add a key value pair to a dictionary, you set the value for a new key. See the example below for syntax and function calls.

```
students = {"cdm_001": "John Brude", "cdm_002":
"Bill Gross", "cdm_003": "Max Johnson"}  #
#dictionary of students with their ID as the
#key and name as the value
students["cdm_001"]  # assumes the value John
#Brude
students["cdm_003"] # assumes the value Max
#Johnson for the key
students.keys()  # returns a list of the keys
#["cdm_001", "cdm_002", "cdm_003"]
del ["cdm_001"]  # removes the key, val from
#the dictionary
```

```
students["cdm_004"] = "Harley Zieper"  # adds a
#new student id and name to the dictionary
```

Just like lists, dictionaries can also be multidimensional meaning you can have dictionaries of dictionaries. For example, we could have a dictionary of locations and ocean conditions, although this could better be implemented with the use of classes (a concept we will discuss later).

```
beach_info = {
   "Blackies":  { "wave_height": 3,
                  "water_temp": 68
    }
    "Wedge": { "wave_height": 6, "water_temp":
     67.3 }
}
# gets the wave_height key from the Blackies
#dictionary from beach_info
beach_info['Blackies']['wave_height']  #assumes
#the value 3
```

How do dictionaries work? Well, they map key objects to value objects with a hash value. Valid key objects, such as strings, have hash functions that take the data in a key object and use it to produce an integer hash value. The hash value represents a bucket where a key-value pair is stored.

In computer science, Big O notation is used to describe the worst-case execution time of an algorithm or process. Due to hashing, the bucket will be located within one iteration (O(1) in Big O notation). If the items were stored in a list, we would have to check each item thus decreasing the efficiency (O(n) in which n is the size of the list). Only objects or data types (such as strings) with a hash function are valid keys. If a custom object is designed to be a valid key, it needs to implement the hash function.

Sets

When you are creating a guest list for an event, you only want to add a friend once to the list. You don't want to have repeats of the same person. Sometimes, we run into similar scenarios while programming, and there is a data structure called a set which is an unordered collection with no duplicate elements. You can initialize an empty set by calling the *set()* function, or you can pass in items inside square brackets. You cannot initialize an empty set with empty square brackets since that would initialize a list. The *add* function inserts an item into a set while the *remove* function deletes an item. There is no duplicate data in a set. See the example below for syntax and function.

```
invites = set()
invites.add("Mike")  # set value is {"Mike"}
```

```
invites.add("Mike") # set value is still
#{"Mike"} because no repeats will be added
invites.remove("Mike") # set is not empty

attending = {"Cameron", "Tia", "Jake",
"Isabell"}  # initialize a set with data
attending.add("Tia")  # no repeats, the set
#will remain the same
```

Tuples

A tuple is a sequence data type that enables us to hold multiple pieces of data about some model. An unnamed tuple takes arguments inside parentheses and values can be accessed with an index like in a list since both of these objects are iterables (objects capable of returning each of their members individually). A named tuple is a bit more useful. It is made possible my importing the collections library and creating a custom tuple with labeled properties that can later be called. See the example below for syntax and function.

```
unnamed_tuple = ("BMW", "i8", 357)  # created
#an unnamed tuple for a car with the brand,
#model, and horsepower
```

```
print(unnamed_tuple[0])  # output is BMW, the #
#first element of the tuple
```

It's very important you import the *collections* package, a library of prewritten code built into the Python Standard Library, before creating a named tuple. First, we must template our named tuple by giving it a name, and setting the properties by passing them in as a list argument. In accordance with Python conventions, the first letter in our tuple name should (although it is not required) be capitalized. When we use our newly created tuple, the first property is unlabeled, but subsequent properties are. We access each value in a tuple by referencing its attribute.

```
# named tuples are more useful because unnamed
# are like lists
# to use a named tuple, you must import the
#collections library to use the namedtuple
#function.
import collections
Car = collections.namedtuple('Car', ['make',
'hp', 'price'])  # creates the structure for
#our custom tuple
lenos_car = Car("BMW", hp=357, price=120000) #
```

```
#first value passed in, subsequent values are
#labeled
print(lenos_car.price)  # outputs 120000
print(lenos_car.make)  # outputs BMW
```

Conclusion

Variables and data structures are an essential component of computer science and application development. Planning your programs and truly understanding the code will enable you to make critical design choices, write clean code, and make your programs efficient. I highly encourage you to re-read this chapter and try coding the examples in IDLE. Also, consider creating your own data structures, playing with various operations, and outputting the result to your screen. You can't just read this book; you must practice to retain the material and develop a thorough understanding. Please make sure you understand data types, lists, and other basic structures before proceeding to new material.

Ch. 2 Conditional Statements

If/else Statements and Boolean Algebra

Programs need a way to make decisions based on the data they are provided, input, or operation of the application. Without the ability to make decisions according to conditions, programs would not be as useful as they are today. For example, a smart thermostat wouldn't be able to start the AC when the air temperature is at sixty-five degrees. In everyday life, the human brain analyzes conditional situations and responds accordingly. When a car approaches a stop light, the driver checks the color of the light. If it is red, they respond by stopping, but if it is green, they respond by maintaining their speed. Alternately, if the light is yellow, they slowly brake to decelerate the car.

Conditional statements use Boolean algebra, a branch of mathematics that is used to analyze logic circuits using only binary to evaluate a scenario. To check a condition, one structure that is commonly used is called an if-statement, but there are other structures in programming including switches. A Boolean expression is a condition that is checked that either returns true or false. Conditionals are what make programs “smart,” and give them the ability to “make decisions”. On a low-level, it's all about whether a bit should be assigned a 1 or a 0 in performing a computational task.

Simple Boolean Algebra

Aristotle, a Greek philosopher, created a two-mode logic system in which a condition is either true or false. His work led to the creation of four primary laws of logic: the Law of Non-Contradiction, the Law of the Excluded Middle, the Law of Identity, and the Law of Rational Interface. These laws apply when a condition is entirely true or entirely false, but don’t quite apply to conditions that are true or false to a limited degree. In 1854, George Boole, an English Mathematician, wrote a publication titled An Investigation of the Laws of Thought, on Which Are Founded the Mathematical Theories of Logic and Probabilities. This publication founded Boolean algebra by creating rules to describe the relationship between mathematical quantities that assume the values true (represented with 1) or false (represented with 0). Also, called binary algebra or logic algebra, we will be using Boolean expressions in the conditional statements coming up in this chapter. Here is a table outlining the resultant Boolean after evaluating the result of one condition and another condition.

condition	operation	result
True and True	and	True
True and False	and	False
False and True	and	False
False and False	and	False
True or True	or	True
True or False	or	True
False or True	or	True
False or False	or	False
not False	not	True
not True	not	False

In circuit design, Boolean conditions are often written in mathematical expressions in which 0 represents false, 1 represents true, an addition symbol represents OR, and a multiplication symbol represents AND. Here are some very basic expressions:

1 + 0 + 1 = 1 (True or False or True is True)

1 x 1 x 1 = 1 (True and True and True is True)

To see some examples of Boolean expressions, try the following example below:

```
print(5==3)  # outputs False
print(2==20)  # outputs False
print(not 5==(4+1))  # outputs False
print((4*2) == 8 and 6==(7-1))  # outputs True
print((4*2) == 9 or 6==5) # outputs False
```

If statements

You often need a control structure that will only run a block of code upon a particular condition being met. An if statement enables us to check a Boolean expression and perform an operation if the condition is met. To use an if statement, you first write the keyword *if*, then add a condition, and then denote the statement with a colon. All the code you would like to be executed for that condition goes under the if statement in an indented code block. In other languages, such as C++ or Java, code for the body of an if statement goes inside curly braces, but we don't use curly braces in Python – we strictly focus on indentation. Optionally, the condition of an if statement can be written inside a set of parenthesis. Here is how to structure an if statement.

```
if expression:
    # code goes inside here
    # indent each line of code that goes inside
```

Let's see an example of how this might be used.

```
country = "US"
if country == "US":
    print("Go America!")
```

Since country equals US, the condition is met, the evaluated expression returns true, and "Go America!" will be output in the console. If the country was equal to Canada or another location, then no message would be output. We can handle a condition that isn't met by using an else statement. If the first condition isn't met, the else block is executed to perform an alternate action. See the next example for the syntax. Notice that the else statement is at the same indentation level as the key word *if*, the word *else* is immediately followed by a colon, and code for the else block is indented.

```
if country == "US":
    print("Go America!")  # either this print
statement or the one below be output
```

```
else:
    print("Go some other country!")  # notice
#that else is at the same indentation was the
#word if and the code we want to execute for
#the else is indented
```

To check multiple conditions, we use an if-elif control structure. Else if, referred to as *elif* in Python, checks for an additional condition until one is met or all conditions are exhausted. After one condition is true, the code for the block is executed, and the if statement is broken out of. This means any other conditional checks are not evaluated. We can chain as many *elif* statements together as we would like to. If no condition is true, we can optionally include an else statement to serve as a catch-all. Below is the syntax for an *if-elif* structure.

```
if condition1:
    # code for condition1 here
elif condition2:
    # code for condition2 here
elif condition3:
    # code for condition3 here
else:
```

```
    # code for no conditions here - else is optional
```

The previous example has an else statement added to the end. This construct is not required, but it will be executed if no previous condition is met. Notice how each conditional check is at the same indentation level and the code that should be executed for that condition should be indented under the check. You must have code within the block for each conditional check or you will receive an error. To temporarily make the *if-elif* structure work, you could insert the *pass* keyword in the code block.

Nested Conditionals

Conditional statements can also be embedded or nested inside other conditional statements. It's important that you monitor your indentation with nested conditionals to ensure that the correct control statements are at the proper outer or inner indentation for the intended logic. Subsequently following is an example of how conditionals can be nested.

```
# assume time is a valid string and hour is a
#value from 0 to 24
if time == "day":
```

```
    if hour > 12:
        print("it's afternoon")     # prints when
#daytime and past 12
        if day == "monday":
            print("It's a monday afternoon")    #
#prints when daytime, past 12, and monday
    elif hour < 12:
        print("it's morning")  # prints when
#daytime and morning
```

When working with nested conditionals, it's important to note that the code in the outer scope of which a nested condition is met will also be executed. With the example above, if it was daytime, a Monday, and the hour was greater than twelve, the following two statements would be output because the first, second, and third condition are all met:

```
>>> it's afternoon
>>> It's a monday afternoon
```

Instead of using a nested control statement, the code in the example could alternately be written with a single if statement in which the condition checks if it is daytime and the hour of the day is greater than twelve. This is a matter of design choice. If you have many conditions that depend on one set of conditions first evaluating to true, then nested control structures may be advantageous, but due to the brevity of the example above, a single if statement with a different Boolean expression would be manageable.

Conclusion

Control structures are essential to make our code respond to user input, environment variables, or any other directives. With Boolean algebra, we can combine conditions together to limit the execution of a block of code. Conditionals can be continually nested in each other, but after two to three levels of nesting, it begins to get messy. If-else control structures are not just found in Python. They are used in almost every programming language. I highly encourage you to try the examples in this chapter and fully understand simple Boolean expressions before moving forward in this book. We have just scratched the surface of Boolean algebra, but it's a branch of mathematics that is vital and widely used in electronics design, circuits, and programming.

Ch. 3 Loops
For and While Loops

When programmers need to perform repeat tasks in code, they usually use two additional control structures: a *for* loop or a *while* loop. Loops are commonly used in large applications, and they are prevalent in a plethora of other languages. They keep programmers from writing repetitive code and are a fantastic means of minimizing your code output. *While* loops continue executing a block of code as long as a condition is true. An infinite loop is a *while* loop that never ends, thus taking up all the available memory on your computer and causing the program to crash. *For* loops are used to iterate over a set of data, particularly a list, or any other iterable object.

Conditional statements can be nested inside loops to perform additional operations on each iteration (pass through) of the loop. Just like the code of a conditional must be indented, the code block you want to be repeated must also be indented under the loop declaration. An example of how a loop may be practically applied in an application is to iterate over all a user's friends on Facebook and determine if they are online or offline.

While Loops

Since while loops execute code if a condition is true, it's very important you have a condition that can end the loop to avoid creating an infinite loop that crashes your program. To write a while loop, you first use the keyword *while*, then write a Boolean expression, and then add a colon. All the code you want to loop to continue running is indented under the while statement.

```
while condition:
    # code to be repeated goes here
```

One way to end a while loop is for the condition to be negated after a threshold is met (such as an item count), or a user command is entered. For example, the code below uses a counter to end the while loop after it has reached the value 100.

```
# Loop will output the number 0 to 99 in the
console
i = 0
while i < 100:
    print(i) # prints i
    i = i + 1  # increments i by 1 for each pass
#by the Loop
```

The example above will print the numbers 0 to 99 and add one to *i* on each iteration of the loop. On the first iteration, 0 is printed and *i* obtains the value of 1. On the second iteration, 1 is printed and *i* obtains the value of 2. This process continues until *i* is 100, the point in which it is no longer less than 100 so the Boolean condition is false. We can end a loop iteration early by using a break statement. When called, a break statement skips the remaining code in the while statement and stops the loop.

```
i = 0
while i < 50:
    i = i + 1
    if i > 20:
        break  # will skip the rest of the loop
when i is 21 or more
    print(i)
```

In the example above, after *i* assumes the value 21, it is no longer printed because the break statement skips the remainder of the loop and stops it. Break statements can be useful to stop infinite loops and to continue performing a task until a value is returned or an action is performed. For example, sometimes the condition for the loop will always be true, and you will need to use a break statement to exit the loop or a return statement if the loop is inside of a function.

Why might this be useful? One use case is when you want to continue asking a user to enter a positive number and keep asking them until they enter a valid value.

```
while True:
    num = input("enter a positive number:")
    if int(num) > 0:
        break
```

The example above keeps asking the user to enter a number until they finally enter one greater than zero at which point they break out of the loop. How would this work inside of a function? It's quite useful. Let's say you have a function in which you ask the user to enter a name and you want to ensure they don't leave it blank.

```
def user_name():
    while True:
        name = input("Enter your name:")
        if len(name) > 0:
            return name
name = user_name()
```

The previous example keeps prompting the user to enter a name until the length of the value is greater than zero.

When this condition is met, the function returns the name entered thus ending the loop and the function call. The variable name below the function definition assumes the value returned by the function.

For loops

It's useful to be able to iterate over a set of data, such as the letters of a word or items of a list, to compare items or perform a function. For loops are used in Python to go through a list of data such as a list of numbers or any iterable object. If we want to repeat a function for a series of numbers, we can generate a list for a starting value to an ending value with the *range* function . The function takes two parameters: a start value that is inclusive an end value that is exclusive (not included in the generated list). See the example below for syntax and function.

```
total = 0  # variables the tracks the sum
for i in range(0, 100):
    total = total +  i  # adds each item to the
#total
print(total)  # outputs the summation of all
#the numbers from 0 to 99
```

In the example, the variable *i* takes on the value of each item in the list generated by the *range* function as it passes through the loop. It doesn't have to be called *i* – it can be named anything meaningful. Notice we denote a for loop with a colon, and all the code that will be repeated with each loop iteration is indented underneath. In the example, the range function returns a list of integers from 0 to 99. Let's examine another example of a for loop.

```
friends=[("Johnny Brown", 9493436565),
("Jackson Jensen", 9492341212), ("Grace
Grippo", 9495243464)]  # list of friend tuples

# outputs name and number for each friend in
#the list
for friend in friends:
    print(friend[0] + " - " + friend[1])
```

It's important to understand that the friend variable in the example above assumes each subsequent value in the friends list with each loop iteration. That means the name of the friend is "Johnny Brown" on the first iteration, "Jackson Jensen" on the second iteration, and "Grace Grippo" on the third iteration.

Nested For Loops

Just as any other control structure can be nested, we can have multiple for loops embedded in each other. Nested for loops are often used when iterating through a multidimensional list to reach all data points. See the example below for structure and syntax:

```
# List of tuples that contain a club name and
list of members
club_roosters = [("NHS", ["John", "Harley",
"Michael", "Sarah", "Chloe", "Annabelle"]),
("Pal", ["Isaac", "Stephanie", "Jamie",
"Glenn"]), ("AGS", ["Kalia", "Sam", "Parker",
"Jake"])]
# iterate through each club tuple
for club in club_roosters:
    print(club[0] + ": ")  # print the name of
#the tuple
    for name in club[1]:  # iterate through the
#list of members in the club tuple
        print(name)  # print the name of each
#member
    print("----") # denote the end of a list of
#members with dashes
```

In the previous example, nested for loops are used to first access each club tuple (NHS, Pal, and AGS) in the list of clubs and then output each member existent within a club tuple. For each iteration of the outer loop, there are n iterations of the inner loop – n is a value dependent on the length of the list (length of club [1] in the example).

Conclusion

Loops are important because they allow as to perform a multitude of operations on large lists of data. They also keep us from writing repetitive code by continuing a command until the condition is invalid. In web applications, loops are often used to iterate over a database of users or continually query data. Loops are also an essential component of game development, where they may be used to continuously spawn several enemies. Just like other control structures, loops check a Boolean expression, and they can be nested within each other. It's important that while loops have a means of ending to avoid an infinite loop that will cause your program to crash.

Ch. 4 Functions
Functions, Arguments, and Return Types

It's important that code is robust, reusable, and human readable which is why we need functions – encapsulated blocks of code. Functions allow code to be reused without having to type it out multiple times, and they can be written in external files outside your main application file to keep your program from getting cluttered. They can also be used in future programs you write to save time and effort from writing code that is already existent for common application tasks such as saving files. Functions usually define an action, and they can accept input, return output, or return *None* (a data type for nothing).

Separating the actions of a program into reusable chunks makes your program more modular and easier to debug. If you find that your program is failing at a function call, you can narrow down the debugging process to the implementation of that function. We've already encountered several built-in Python functions including *print* and *input*. We simply call these functions and provide arguments, but their underlying implementation is hidden from us. They are descriptive (it's rather obvious by the name what *print* does), and they allow us to think about the high order of our program implementation rather than worrying about the underlying details. Functions such as *print* are also useful because we use them repeatedly in our code.

Function Structure

A function (reusable code block) is created using the Python keyword *def* and providing the name of the function along with a set of parenthesis. This statement must be demarcated by a colon, and any of the code within the function must be indented underneath (like how the code in an if statement is indented). Functions should be given a short yet descriptive name and start with lowercase letters. For multiword names, each word should be separated with an underscore.

```
def function_name():
    # code goes here indented
    print("this is a function")
```

In the example above, we have defined a function, meaning we have named it. We have also implemented it by writing code inside the function. If this were in your Python file and you ran the program, nothing would happen – the statement "this is a function" would not be output. This occurs because a function needs to be called for it to be executed. It's like a coffee machine – it's sitting there to perform an action, but it is only used when you insert a pod and start the machine. To call a function somewhere in you program, you type out the name of the function exactly synonymous to its declaration, and you add a set of parenthesis. For example, this is how we would call the function from the last function declaraction:

```
# the function implementation isn't shown
# this is my main code file
function_name()  # the function has been called
#and the print statement will output
```

Any code that you would write outside a function can be encapsulated inside of one. You can have if-else statements, for loops, while loops, variables, and anything else you would like to in the implementation of a function. All the code inside a function has its own local namespace (the scope where a variable or function exists). If we declare a new variable inside a function, this would have what is referred to as local scope and the variable wouldn't be accessible outside the function. The next example demonstrates scope.

```
# main file - global scope
num1 = 20
```

```
def test_function():
    # num2 has local scope - I can't reference
#it outside the function
    num2 = 55

# I can reference num1 because it can be
#accessed inside the function
# since it has global scope
num1 = 33
```

Namespaces

A namespace is usually implemented in Python as a dictionary. It is a mapping between names and objects. These mappings are handled by the Python interpreter, and it affects the way you access Python objects. Examples of namespaces include the built-in functions in Python such as the *input* function, modules, and classes. Attributes are references to names, and they are followed by a dot. An attribute may be an object in a module or a property of a class. For example, after importing the math module, *sin* is an attribute of the math module in the statement *math.sin*. Some attributes in modules or classes are read-only, meaning they cannot be assigned values. Each namespace has a different life cycle, but local namespaces are created upon the function call and deleted when the function is done executing. The scope , which we referred to earlier, is the area in a program in which a namespace can be accessed. When a variable or object has global scope, it can be accessed anywhere in a Python module or through an interactively running program. Namespaces follow a hierarchy. An example of a local scope would be the area within a function. When a variable in the local and global scope have the same name, the local scope takes precedence over the global one. You must use the keyword *global* if you want to modify the global variable when it also exists locally. For example:

```
a1 = 5
b1 = 10
def test():
    global a1
    a1 = 3
    b1 = 5
    print(b1)
test()
```

When you call the test function in the example above, *a1* is 5 before the function and *b* is 10. After the call, *b1* is still 10, but the local value of *b1,* the number 5, is printed since the local scope takes precedence over the global value.

Since *a1* is globally modified with the keyword *global*, its value is 3 after the function call. If the global *a1* initialization was not existent, a local variable *a1* would be added to the function namespace, but *a1* wouldn't have been modified globally so it would have retained the value 5 after the function call. It's generally bad to modify global values inside a function, but in the rare instances that you do need to do so, you must first declare the variable on a line with the keyword *global* before you can assign it a value.

Return Types

Most of the time, we want a function to return a value rather than perform a generic operation or modify a global variable. Return statements cause a function to yield an answer that can later be used in a program or assigned to a variable. The return type is the data type of the content being returned. For example, some functions return strings, integers, or lists. Functions that do not return a value implicitly return a *NoneType* object, indicating that it has no value. For a function to yield a value, you add the keyword *return* along with the variable or value you wish to output. See the subsequent example for structure and syntax.

```
# example of a function that returns a string
def get_secret():
    return “shazam”
```

```
word = get_secret()  # shazam string returned
#and assigned to variable
print(word) # output variable value in console
```

The *return* keyword is generally the last line of a function, but you can also have a *return* statement inside of a conditional or loop. Here is an example of a return statement inside of an if statement:

```
attempts = 5
def get_secret():
    if attempts > 4: # if this condition is met,
shazam is never returned
        return “too many attempts”
    return “shazam”

word = get_secret()  # since attempts = 5, too
many attempts is returned
print(word)
```

Arguments

You often need the ability to pass values into a function for an operation to be performed without having to use a global variable. Arguments (also referred to as parameters) are values that are passed into a function to be executed upon. They are like a variable that is passed into a function since they follow the same naming convention and data types. The scope of arguments is limited to the function they are defined for. When using them, they are passed inside the parenthesis of a function definition, and there is no limit on the number of parameters that can be passed into the function. To add multiple parameters, you simply separate them with commas. See the example below for structure and function.

```
# example function with parameters that gets
#profit margin
# parameters - revenue, expenses
def get_margin(revenue, expenses)
    result = (revenue - expenses)/revenue
    return result
# the input arguments are positional
margin = get_margin(500000, 210000)
```

In the example above, *revenue* would be assigned the value 500000 when the function is called and *expenses* would obtain the value 210000. The arguments are named *revenue* and *expenses* so that it's easy to understand the implementation of the function, but they can be named anything like a variable. Theoretically, they could be called r and e. In other languages, parameters are often passed by value or passed by reference. A parameter is passed by reference when a variable is passed directly into a function and the argument is essentially an alias for the variable passed in. Both the parameter and variable passed in point to the same location in memory, thus changing the value of the parameter also changes the value of the variable. A variable is passed by value when a function receives a copy of the arguments and these are stored in a new location in memory. As a result, changing the value of the parameter wouldn't change the value of the original variable passed in. Python is different – it's what we refer to as pass by object. This means a function receives a reference to the same object in memory of the variable that is passed in, but the function creates a new variable for itself like a pass by value situation.

Named Arguments

In the introduction to arguments above, we examined positional arguments in which we pass values in the order that the function arguments have been defined. Sometimes, to make code more human readable or to create optional values, we use named arguments, meaning they are labeled. They are defined like normal parameters except they are assigned a default value which also means they don't have to be included in the function call. See the example below for structure and syntax.

```
# named parameters example
# default values are set for the labeled
#arguments
def check_divisibility(dividend = 1,
divisor=1):
    if dividend % divisor == 0:
        return True
    return False

# example of how the function is called
divisible = check_divisibility(dividend=63,
divisor=9)
```

Nested Functions

Functions can be embedded within functions to hide their scope and make them only accessible to the outer function in which they are called. This essentially masks them from the global scope, but nested functions can also be used to perform preliminary checks on data before it is passed into another function. For example, you may have a program that calculates the net force of an object given a mass and acceleration. It could be useful to first have a function that does a preliminary check on the argument passed in to ensure it's a valid positive value and then call an embedded function to carry out the calculation. Checking the data helps prevent the program from crashing when a user erroneously enters a negative value for mass. Here is an example:

```
# function that finds force with f=ma
def net_force(mass, acceleration):
    # simple embedded function
    def force_calc():
        return mass * acceleration
    if not mass == 0:
        force_calc()
```

Args and Kwargs

Sometimes, we want the ability to pass in a varying number of arguments into a function. For example, maybe we are writing a function that takes in students as arguments and randomly selects one to be called on. In another case, maybe we are making an http request to an API and the number of parameters we need for the request varies. A list of arguments, denoted with*args,* is used to pass a non-keyworded list of parameters into a function. A key-worded argument list, denoted with ***kwargs*, is used to pass in a variable length dictionary of arguments. Let's first examine an example function that uses **args*.

```
def args_test(a, *args, **kwargs):
    print(a) # a is a normal positional argument
```

```
    for arg in args:
        print(arg)
args_test("normal", "arg-1","arg-2", "arg-3",
test="1 key word arg", test2="2 key word args")
```

In the example above, *a* is a normal positional argument, but then we pass in additional parameters that end up being stored in a list called *args*. We also have a **kwargs* argument that allows us to pass in a variable number of labeled parameters. In this case, *test* and *test2* are added to the **kwargs* list in the function call. The function prints out the contents of the *args* list, meaning it would output the following:

```
>>> arg-1
>>> arg-2
>>> arg-3
```

Although we generally name argument lists **kwargs* or **args* depending on their structure, these arguments can be named anything as long as a single asterisk is appended to the beginning of the name for a list of arguments, and two asterisks are appended for a key worded argument list.

Recursion

The action of a function calling itself is known as recursion, and it is helpful for certain repetitive, algorithmic processes such as calculating the factorial of a number. As a reminder, the factorial of a number is a number multiplied out by all the integers below it. To write a recursive function that is useful, it's important to define a base case for when the function returns a direct value. The recursive case will continue calling the function until the base case is reached which is why it's important. You don't want a recursive call to continue indefinitely and crash your program like an infinite loop would. Let's examine a program that recursively finds the factorial of a number.

```
def factorial(n):
    if n == 1:      # base case
        return 1
    return n * factorial(n-1)  # recursive
#call
print(factorial(5))   # should output 120
```

The example calls itself to multiply out 5 x 4 x 3 x 2 x 1 and stop the recursive call when n==1 (the smallest digit in a factorial calculation). The example above can also be coded without using recursion (see the subsequent example).

```
    # factorial calculation using loop
    def factorial(n):
        result = 1
        for i in range(1, n+1) # last term of
#range function is not included, so add 1
            result = result * i # multiply by i,
#the incrementing digit
        return result

    print(factorial(6))  # output should be 720
```

Let’s examine another example of recursion by finding the value of a base raised to an exponent. Here’s how it may be implemented recursively:

```
def power(base, exp):
    if exp == 1:
        return base
    return base * power(base, exp-1)
print(power(3, 3)) # output should be 27
```

In the power example, we continually multiply our base by recursively calling the power function. Each time the function is called, the *exp* variable is decreased by one and the base case is eventually met, thus prompting the function to return the result of the calculation. Here's how the function works for base three to the third power:

Number of Calls	base	exp
1	3	3
2	9	2
3	27	1
4	The result, 27, returned	1

Now let's examine how we could implement a power function using a loop instead of recursion.

```
def power(base, exp):
    result = 1
    for i in range(1, exp+1):
        result = result * base  # keeps
multiplying the base by itself
    return result
print(power(3, 3))  # output should be 27
```

In the example above, you may be wondering why we increment the variable *exp* by one when using the range function. Just to recap, the first term of the range function is inclusive while the last term is exclusive. What this means is if we call the range function with a start value of one and end value of five, this will only generate a list of the numbers one through four. If we intend to include the number five in the list, we must add one to the end value just as we do in the example above.

Conclusion

To abstract our code and make it more manageable, the use of functions in large programs is imperative. They can make our code more modular and reusable. With the use of arguments, both labeled and positional, they can perform virtually any operation assuming it has been correctly implemented and called. Abstracting our code into functions also enables us to hide the underlying implementation when writing an application. Functions can be embedded, call themselves recursively, return nothing, or return a value that can later be used. Each function has its own local scope and namespace, where its parameters are available and other defined variables.

Ch. 5 Classes
Object Oriented Programming

With our exercises up to this point, we've been using a functional programming paradigm or pattern in Python. For practicality purposes, it's generally easier to think of data in terms of objects and actions which is why we will be examining object oriented programming (OOP), a popular paradigm used by languages such as Java and C++. What's unique about Python is that it is a multi-paradigm language, while others are exclusively object oriented, imperative, functional, or declarative. Previously, we have examined Python's default object types such as strings, lists, and integers, but classes enable us to instantiate our own custom objects with properties and actions.

Object oriented programming is another layer of abstraction that makes our code more reusable, readable, and modular. For example, if we are creating an airline point of sale system in Python, we may represent items such as tickets, passengers, planes, and flights with objects. It's more intuitive than using dictionaries and a mix of functions we define collectively to perform operations on data. It's critical you understand classes, objects, inheritance, and other OOP concepts so pay special attention to this chapter.

What is a class?

A class is a blueprint for creating an object, and it is defined with the keyword *class*. Inside, we define class attributes and methods – functions that act upon an object and belong to a class. A constructor is a method that initializes an object, and each class has one by default. We also can define our own constructors that can take parameters to assign them to the attributes of a class. Here is the basic syntax to create a class:

```
class Name:
    def __init__(self, arg1):  # example
#constructor
        self.arg1 = arg1 # example attribute
#assignment
    def test_method:
        return self.arg1 # example method
```

Classes are defined using the keyword *class* and then providing a name as seen above. Although you don't have to, it's recommended that you begin a class name with a capital letter and any other words in a multi-word name also have a capitalized letter at the beginning. This is slightly different from camel casing, in which the first letter of the first word isn't capitalized and the beginning letters of subsequent words are. Each class has its own namespace and methods that we can call on instances of that class. The constructor is defined with two underscores, the keyword *init*, and two additional underscores. You pass the keyword *self* as an argument to the constructor, but it also can accept other arguments. We will learn more about constructors later in this chapter.

What is an Object?

An object is an instance of a class with its own properties and methods. For example, if a class is like a blueprint for a car, defining its properties and actions, then the object is like the actual car that is built in accordance with the blueprint. It receives its own engine, identification number, color, performance packages, and other properties. If another car is manufactured, it also belongs to the car class but will have its own unique identification number, engine, and attributes. To create an object, you simply call the constructor of a class. For example, let's say the *Car* class exists in our program and has previously been defined, then we would create an object like this:

```
# uses default constructor, but we could assign
#attributes declared
```

```
# in the class such as brand or model
example_car = Car()
```

Now that we've created an object, we can call defined methods on this object and modify its attributes. Optionally, we can instantiate another car object to represent a different car. Assuming that the following properties and methods have previously been defined in the *Car* class, let's see an example.

```
carA = Car()
carA.brand = "Mercedes"  # brand is an
#attribute of the car class
carA.go_forward() # go forward is a method
carB = Car()
carB.brand = "BMW"
carB.go_forward()
```

Constructors

When we instantiate an object in Python, a default constructor is often used to create it. A constructor is like an initialization method that sets up a new object and stores it in our computer's memory. Sometimes, we want to define our own custom constructors or override the default class constructor to perform an additional operation upon the initialization of an object. Using the car example, let's say we want to override the default constructor. Here's what we would do:

```
class Car:
    def __init__(self):
        self.car_started = False
```

By default, when a car object is instantiated it will have the *car_started* property set to *False*. We also can set additional properties or call defined functions in the constructor. A custom constructor can be used to accept arguments upon the creation of an object that can be used to set its attributes. For example, if you want to specify the year and brand when creating a car object, you could do the following:

```
class Car:
    def __init__(self, brand, year):
        self.brand = brand  # sets class property
#to the value of the argument
        self.year = year
```

To initialize a car object with the custom constructor, you would do the following:

```
car1 = Car("Mercedes", 2014)  # custom
#constructor
```

```
car1.year = 2015 # still can change properties

car2 = Car() # default constructor
car2.brand="Tesla" # still can set properties
```

Constructors With Optional Arguments

In languages such as Java, you can overload constructors by writing duplicate copies that each accept different arguments. In Python, overloading is not an acceptable practice. If you need a constructor with varying arguments, you should use named arguments, *args, or *kwargs. Here is an example of how you could use a named argument to optionally accept a car model:

```
class Car:
    def __init__(self, brand, model=None):
        self.brand = brand
        if model != None:
            self.model = model
```

In the example above, a single constructor in the car class accepts a positional argument to represent a brand and an optional argument to represent a model. If the object that is being instantiated overrides the model argument by passing a value into the constructor, then model will no longer equal *None* so the model property will be set for this class inside the *if* statement.

```
carA = Car("Audi")  # only takes the positional
# argument
print(carA.brand)  # outputs Audi

carB = Car("Ford", "Fusion") # sets the
# optional model argument
print(carB.model) # outputs Fusion
```

Methods

Functions that are called upon an object are known as methods in object oriented programming. Inside our classes, we can define our own methods in the namespace of the class using the same conventions we use while defining a function. Methods, just like functions, can accept arguments, contain loops or other constructors, and can return a value. Make sure that when you define the method for a class you pass in the keyword *self* which represents the current instance of the class. Let's see an example of a stop method in the car class. Assume all properties and function calls are valid implementations.

```
class Car:
    def __init__(self, brand):
        self.brand = brand

    # stop method
    def stop(self):
        self.accelerator_power = 0
        self.apply_brakes()

    # example of a method to set cruise control
    def cruise_control(self, speed=0)
        self.speed = speed
```

In the example above, we've defined a stop method that takes no arguments (besides self), and we've also defined a cruise control method that accepts a single labeled argument. Here's an example of how we might call these functions:

```
car = ("Ferrari")
car.cruise_control(speed=75)

# assume stop_approaching is a valid boolean
if (stop_approaching == True):
```

```
    car.stop() # self is implicitly passed to
#the stop function
```

Functions With Optional Arguments

In the same way we can have constructors with named arguments, we can also have methods or functions with these arguments that behave differently depending on the arguments passed in. For example, you may have a function named *calc_volume,*. You may want to accept various arguments so that one time it can calculate the volume of a cylinder another time it can find the volume of a cube. One case might only need a radius and a height as arguments while another case may simply take in a side length. Here's an example:

```
# volume of cylinder
# r - radius, h - height, s - side
def volume(r=None, h=None, s=None):
    if s != None:
        return s**3
    elif r != None and h != None:
        return math.pi * (r**2) * h
```

```
# example function calls
cylinder = volume(r=1, h=5)  # #returns 5*pi
cube = volume(s=2) # returns 8
```

Inheritance

In object oriented programming, inheritance is a concept that enables us to create subclasses from base classes to have access to the attributes of a base class yet add to those properties in our own class. Inheritance creates a hierarchy of class relationships, each with a narrower or broader scope than the other. Inheritance can be demonstrated with an example – animals. We may a base class called *Animal* in which there are other classes that inherit from the *Animal* class such as a fish or mammal class. The lower classes in the hierarchy, such as *Sailfish* and *Billfish*, can access attributes and methods from the classes above it or override them. The *Billfish* class can access a property in the *Fish* or *Animal* class, but not in the *Sailfish* class because it's the superclass of it. A superclass is a parent of another class, while a subclass is a child of that parent. In the next chart, the *Animal* class would be a super class for *Mammal*, *Carnivore*, and *Lion* – all of which are considered subclasses. Reference the hierarchy chart to view the relationship.

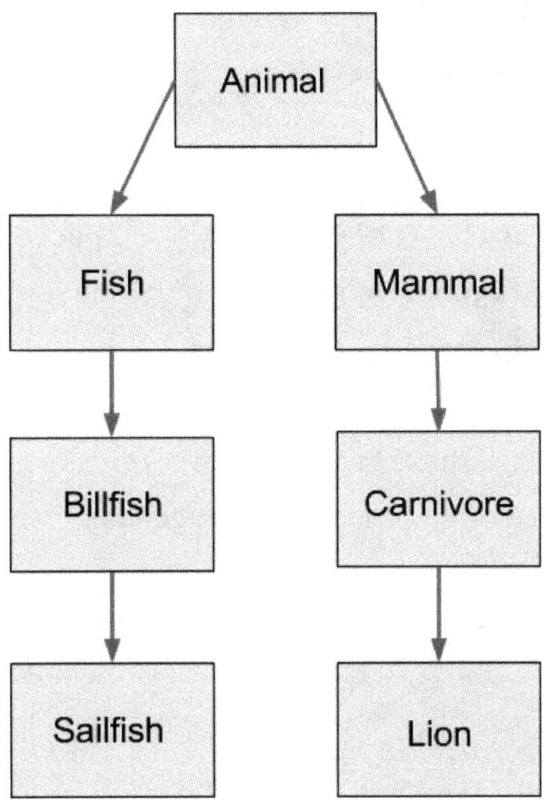

Inheritance is a common phenomenon, and there are no limits to the depth of the hierarchy. It denotes relationships between objects. If used efficiently, it keeps programmers from writing repetitive code. See the next example of how inheritance may work with the classes shown in the chart above.

```
# superclass
class Animal:
    multicellular = True
    dna = True

    def __init__(self, genus="", species=""):
        self.genus = genus
        self.species = species

    def get_classification(self):
        return {"genus": self.genus, "species":
self.species}

# subclass of Animal
# attributes, methods, and constructor are
#inherited
class Carnivore(Animal):
    def __init__(self, diet=[]):
        super.init(self)
        self.diet = diet
```

```
    def output_diet(self):
        for item in diet:
            print(item)

# subclass of Carnivore
# can access namespace of Carnivore class and
Animal class
class Lion(Carnivore):
    def __init__(self, pride="", location="",
foods=[]):
            super(Lion,
self).__init__(diet=foods) #can use the
constructor in the parent class
        self.pride = pride
        self.location = location

    def get_pride(self):
        return self.pride


l = Lion(pride="ubuntu", location="South
Africa")
print(l.dna)  # outputs True (value defined in
#Animal class)
```

```
print(l.get_pride()) # outputs the pride name
#ubuntu
```

In the previous example, the statement *super(class name, self.init* is used to call a constructor in the parent class. In the case of the *Lion* class, the constructor of the *Carnivore* class is called so that the diet could be defined upon instantiating the object. Calling the constructor of a parent class is entirely optional. You can just call the constructor for the class you are instantiating or the default empty constructor.

Polymorphism

Objects may appear in many forms as we've seen with the various types of classes we have previously defined, but some of these objects share common actions or attributes. Polymorphism is the ability to access multiple objects with the same function or call the same method upon multiple objects. Here is one example of polymorphism:

```
class Audi(Car):
    def start(self):
        print("Vroom! Car started")
Class Whaler(Boat):
    def start(self):
```

```
        print("dudududu, boat running")

# start can validly be called on an Audi object
#or Whaler object
def start_it(device):
    device.start()
start_it(Audi())
start_it(Whaler())
```

What is useful about polymorphism is that we can access functions or properties without worrying about the type of an object. In the example above, we may have a function that starts a device and we just want it to call a valid start function. We don't really care about the type as long as there is a valid start function definition and implementation.

Conclusion

Programming paradigms are important for designing programs in an intuitive manner to represent data and actions. The Object-Oriented Programming (OOP) paradigm is commonly used in large applications and across various languages including Java and C++. Representing data in terms of objects simplifies the process of understanding how a program works. It can be more efficient to use object relationships and inheritance to avoid writing repetitive code.

OOP is also reusable since you can rapidly create new instances of a class, it adds a layer of abstraction, and it's an effective means of organizing your code.

Ch. 6 Handling Files

Basics File Operations

It's time to take our code to a new dimension by learning about basic file operations. Files enable us to store external data that can be accessed or written to. They can contain text, audio content, CSV (comma separated values) content, or another format. We can use them as a means of persisting data or loading data into a structure for manipulation or analysis such as a multidimensional list. In the following chapter, we are going to learn about opening files, reading their content, and writing to them, mainly with text files and CSVs.

Built-in Python functions enable us to work with files, but the *csv* module can also be used to easily manipulate data in csv files. The basic idea is to open a file with the appropriate permissions, call the appropriate methods upon the file object, and close the file when we are done reading from it or writing to it.

Reading Text Files

The first step in reading a text file is opening the file. To do this, the *open* function is called with the file path as a required argument and the mode as an optional argument. Here is the structure of the open function call:

```
# filename = location + name (ex.
#/desktop/test.txt)
file = open(filepath, mode)
```

Make sure you know the *filepath* argument is the location of the file relative to the project directory or it's the absolute path. For example, if you have a project directory with a folder named *files* which contains a file named *test.txt*, you could enter */files/test.txt* for the file path. Alternatively, you could enter the absolute file path (full path to the file location) which may be something like */Users/YOUR_NAME/ documents/project/files/test.txt* (path on a Mac). To find the absolute file path, open a shell, cd into the directory of your file, and type the *pwd* command which stands *for print working directory*. The next table contains valid mode arguments if it's optionally passed into the *open* function. There are multiple constructors for the open function so the mode isn't necessarily required, but I recommend you provide one so that your program functions with the intended permissions.

Argument	Permissions
‘r’	File is only read
‘w’	Edit or write new information to the file
‘a’	Append (add new data to the end of the file)
‘r+’	Read and write mode

Create a new Python file in IDLE, name it, and save this to a directory on your computer that you can easily access again. Then, open your favorite text editor (or you can open Text Edit on a Mac) and type the following content, each on a separate line as seen below.

```
We can’t help everyone, but
Everyone can help someone.
Ronald Reagan
```

Save the file as *file_text.txt* in the same directory as where you saved your Python file (the Python file and txt file should be in the same folder). Now, transition back to your Python file, and write the following code:

```
f = open(‘file_txt.txt’, ‘r’)
lines = file.readlines()    # returns a list
#containing each line
```

```
first_line = file.readline()  # returns the
#first line
print(file.read(2))   # returns the first 2
#characters read
```

In the example above, after opening the file there are multiple methods we call on the file object to read its content. The first method, *readlines*, returns a list of lines. The returned list would contain the items "*We can't help everyone, but*", "*Everyone can help someone.*", and "*Ronald Reagan*". The next method, *readline*, returns the content of the first line, in this case the string "*We can't help everyone, but*". The last method, *read*, takes an argument with the number of characters we want to get. In this case, passing in the argument two returns the first two characters "*We*". If you don't pass in an argument to the read function, then it returns all the content of the file. What if you want to loop through all the lines in a file? Reference the next example.

```
f = open('file_text.txt', 'r')

# Loops through each line in the file
for line in f:
    print(line)
```

Looping through file lines is useful because it enables as to access the data on each line and perform an intended action. For example, if we had expenditures listed on each line, we could add them together and output a total expenditure. Each line is treated as a string, so you must use string methods to add, remove, or parse the content of each line. For example, let's say we replace all the content in *file_text.txt* with charges on a credit card (each has a date, last four digits, and amount).

```
01/02/2017  4444  45.00
01/09/2017  2323  100.00
01/21/2017  4444  25.00
```

If we wanted to get the total amount spent, we could loop through each line of the file, get the floating-point value at the end, and add this to the total. Notice that in the data above, the last four digits of the card and the amount are separated by spaces. This will allow us to easily extract the content. The *split* function is a method that can be called on a string that divides it at a delimiter and returns a list of separate strings. Calling the *split* function without any arguments divides a string at a space, so the string "one two three" would return a list such as ["one", "two", three"]. By passing in a delimiter into the *split* function, a string can be divided in a different manner. For example, calling *split (",")* would divide a string at comma values so a string such as “s1, s2, s3” would return a list such as [“s1”, “s2”, “s3”]. The example below iterates through charge data in a file, splits each line at the space, and obtains data from the split string.

```
f = open('file_text.txt')
total = 0
for line in file:
    data = line.split()  # splits the string at
#the space
    amount = data[2]  # gets the last item in
#the data list
    total = total + float(amount) # casts to
#float and adds the value
print(total)  # total for the example charges
#should be 170
```

Writing to Files

To write to a file, you must first open it with permission to write or append to it. This is a situation in which you need to pass in a mode argument. If you get permission to write, you will be able to add to the existing content of the file or you can edit it. Appended content is added to the end of the file and doesn’t affect the existing text. Here’s is an example of how you could write to the text file we've previously created in this chapter:

```
file = open('write_text.txt', 'w')
file.write('Bond. James Bond')
file.close()  # frees up resources taken by file
```

Since *write_text.txt* didn't exist, the file should've been created in your main project directory and should contain the string "*Bond. James Bond*". In the example above, we call the close method to free up system resources used by the file once we are done using the file object. Also, now that the file exists, the *open* function will retrieve that file instead of creating a new one. If you try changing the string in the write method and re-run the program, you will notice "*Bond. James Bond*" is overwritten with your new text. If instead you want to add to this text, you could change the file mode to append the new content.

Crash Prevention

The problem with the *open* function is that it can fail if you attempt to read a nonexistent file or a file with an invalid extension. Once it fails, your program will probably crash, but the *with* keyword enables us to try to open a file and only call methods upon the file object if it properly opens. To use this, create a file object, use the *with* keyword, and indent your file code below the *with* statement. See the example below for structure and function.

```
with open('file_text.txt') as f:
    # file object named f (can be any name)
    # code in here is skipped if file open fails
     print(f.read())
```

JSON

JavaScript Object Notation (JSON) is a data format commonly used for storing information in files, storing information in databases, and sending data through network requests. A JSON object, denoted with two curly braces, is a set of name value pairs that are separated by commas. Valid JSON values include numbers, strings, Boolean values, arrays, other JSON objects, or null (which means nothing). This data-interchange format isn't anything Python specific. It's widely used with servers, client programs, and http requests. We are going to learn about handling JSON in Python, but first let's look at an example of some valid JSON objects, so you can understand the structure. Once again, the syntax used for these objects is specific to JSON, not Python.

```
"User": {
    "Id": 5,
    "Name": "Sergey Brin"
    "Hobbies": ["coding", "skiing"]
}
```

In the example above, *User* is a JSON object with three different key-value pairs. The first key-value pair is an id with a number value, the second is a name key with a string value, and the third is a hobbies key with an array of string values. Now that we've learned a little about JSON, let's dive into using Python's *json* module. To properly save JSON data to a file, it must first be encoded. See the example to see how to encode data and save it to a file.

```
import  json  # must import the module at the
top of your code
with open('data_test.txt') as outfile:
    data = {"name": "Howard Schultz",
"position": "CEO", "company":"Starbucks"}
      json.dump(data, outfile)  # dump encodes
the data dic and saves it
```

In the example above, the *data* dictionary is encoded into JSON and saved to a file named *data_test.txt*. Parsing is the process of loading JSON into a dictionary that we can use to reference its data. For example, if after running the example above the file *data_test.txt* exists with valid JSON data, we can parse it by doing the following:

```
import json
with open('data_test.txt') as outfile:
    file_data = outfile.read()  # gets data from
#file
    json_data = json.load(file_data) # parses
#data to dictionary
    name = json_data["name"]  # can now access
#dictionary keys
```

CSV Files

Comma separated values (CSV) files are sometimes used to store spreadsheet content in plain text. As a result, you can convert an excel or numbers spreadsheet into a csv file with relative ease. A delimiter is a symbol that is used to separate data. Since there is no requirement for csv files, the delimiter doesn't have to be a comma. It could be multiple spaces, a dash, or some other symbol, but we are going to assume for the purposes of the next code example that it is a comma. To work with these files, we need to import the *csv* module at the top of our Python code which gives us several methods that make it easy to access and write data. First, let's write an example csv file that we can work with. Open a text editor such as Notepad or Text Edit and write the following:

```
Company, Founding Date, Symbol
Apple, 1976, APPL
Broadcom, 1991, AVGO
SolarCity, 2006, SCTY
```

Save the text file you created as *test.csv* in the main project directory in which you've previously worked with files. Now, here is an example of the structure and function of code that can read from and write to the csv file:

```
import csv  #import the csv module
with open('test.csv') as file:
    reader = csv.reader(file)  #use reader to
#get the file content
    for row in reader:  # for loop will output
#each line in the file
        print(row)  # each row is a list of
#values

    writer = csv.writer(file) # create a writer
#object
    write.writerow(['Starbucks', 1971, 'SBUX'])
    # write to the csv file
```

```
file.close() # important
```

In the previous example, a *reader* object is used to get the content of the file. We can then iterate through the reader object to access the data line by line. We can also create a writer object, which we can use to add a row to the data. It's important we close the file when we are done to ensure it saves properly.

Conclusion

The ability to read and write files is important to add complexity to our programs and enable us to store data externally. You should now be familiar with the basics of working with text files, JSON data, and csv files. JSON is a structure you will continually encounter while working with data and you can learn more about it at json.org. Next time you have a spreadsheet in which you are working with items such as your assignments and grades, you can convert that data to a csv file and write your own Python program to perform calculations or an analysis. Remember, we've just scratched the surface in terms of working with files and data. Reference the Python documentation to see what other methods are available to you and consider looking at Python libraries such as *simplejson*.

Ch. 7 Error Handling and Debugging
Preventing a Crash or Fixing One

Never rely on the users of a program to always do things right because they are going to inevitably make mistakes. Sometimes, the mistakes of a user or a bug in a program can cause it to crash. For example, you may be expecting the user to pass in an integer to a function, but they instead pass in a string. In another instance, a user may try to open a file that doesn't exist or is not readable. Error handling is the process of appropriately responding to potential errors in our code through mistakes such as invalid file reads. We can use a try statement to attempt to execute a block of code and handle potential errors that are thrown.

In Python, we also can create our own errors and initiate them when appropriate. For example, a program may expect data returned from a server to be in an exact format and may raise a custom error if the returned data format is incorrect. The ability to create our own errors is helpful in the debugging process and a crucial part of defining the possible erroneous portions of a program. These custom errors that we define can also be checked by a try statement so that appropriate action is taken if one of our own errors is triggered.

Inevitably, bugs will arise in programs you write especially as the complexity of those programs increases. Debugging is the process of working through errors to fix code that is causing your program to either crash or perform an unintended action. Especially when it comes to the process of locating erroneous code, it's important your code is easy to follow, well commented, and rather intuitive. In this chapter, we will introduce some tips for debugging, and we will outline debugging tools that are built into IDLE.

Exceptions

An exception is an error that is raised when a program is run. You probably have already encountered exceptions in your previous coding mistakes. In the error console, you may have seen a defined error name and description as your program crashed. It may have also shown the line number of the code statement that triggered the error. For example, if you open a Python interactive shell and divide a number by zero, Python raises a *ZeroDivisionError*. Reference the subsequent screenshot of this error.

```
>>> 5/0
Traceback (most recent call last):
  File "<pyshell#41>", line 1, in <module>
    5/0
ZeroDivisionError: division by zero
>>> if {
      }
SyntaxError: invalid syntax
>>> 5 + "3"
Traceback (most recent call last):
  File "<pyshell#44>", line 1, in <module>
    5 + "3"
TypeError: unsupported operand type(s) for +: 'int' and 'str'
>>>
```

The *ZeroDivisionError* is a built-in Python error which you can see above. Other built-in exceptions including the *SyntaxError* and *TypeError* are also demonstrated. Upon executing the last command, a *TypeError* is raised because the code attempts to add an integer to a string, an invalid operation. For this to work properly, the string value of “3” would need to be casted to an integer and then added to the integer five. To stop an error from crashing your program, you must handle the exception. Luckily, we have the try statement to help us in this process.

Try Statement

The try statement is a construct for error handling that can take appropriate action if a block of code fails. It is defined with the keyword *try* followed by a colon. The code we want to attempt to execute should be indented under the try statement definition. Next, we add *except* statements in which we can catch a single exception (a raised error) or multiple different types of exceptions. We must handle a minimum of one exception. In the same manner we can add more *elif* clauses to an if statement to check additional conditions, we can continually add more except clauses to a try statement. Here is an example of a try statement:

```
try:
    file = open('test.txt')
    secret_number =int(file.read())
except FileNotFoundError:
    # this would be run if test.txt wasn't found
    print("Sorry, but test.txt doesn't exist.
Change the file path")
except ValueError:
    # run if casting file content to integer
#failed
     print("secret_number is not a valid
integer")
```

In the code above, the *FileNotFoundError* outputs a message if the *text.txt* file cannot be found. In this case, additional actions can be taken such as taking input for a user to enter a new file path. The *ValueError* is another built-in exception that is raised if the string content of the read file cannot be casted to an integer. Try statements can also handle any general exception that is raised instead of catching a specific error. Here is how your program could catch any error that is raised:

```
try:
    num1 = int("hahaha")
    result  = 5/0
except Exception:
    print("Uh oh, something went wrong")
```

The except clause in the example above is a "catch all" because no matter what type of exception is raised, it will be caught. Even as a *ValueError* is raised or a *ZeroDivisionError*, they are still both caught by the general exception. This can be combined with other except statements as a safeguard against a crash in which you may not have accounted for all the possible exceptions that could be thrown.

The except clause can catch multiple different exceptions that are raised and respond to them in the same manner. This requires less code than chaining multiple except statements as seen in the last example, but there is a disadvantage: the code in the except statement is going to be the same for any of the caught errors. Because of this, it may be more advantageous for a program to have separate except clauses for items such as a *FileNotFoundError* and a *ValueError* so that the program can respond differently to each one. For example, for a *FileNotFoundError*, the program could ask the user to re-enter the filename whereas a *ValueError* could cause a message to be output. To catch multiple exceptions, the keyword *except* is used like any other exception, but then the exceptions that you would like to catch are specified in a set of parenthesis with each item separated by a comma. See the example below for structure and function.

```
try:
     # code to try goes here
     # code such as "3" - "5" would trigger a
#TypeError
     i = 3 + "3"  # this would trigger a value
#error
except (ValueError, TypeError):
    # do something here
     print("There was a value or type error")
```

Finally Clause

Sometimes, we want a block of code that is always executed before leaving the try statement, regardless of whether an exception does or does not occur. This is the job of the finally clause. See the next example for structure and function.

```
try:
    result = int("3")
except Exception:
    print("some exception was caught")
finally:
    print("this is output independent of an
            exception occurring")
```

Else for Try Statements

When examining if statements earlier in this book, we encountered the else clause which can also be used with try statements. If no exception is caught or no exception is initially raised, the else statement will be executed. The else statement should be defined after all the exceptions you would like to handle are defined. See the example below for structure and function.

```
try:
    result  = x/y  # assume x and y are integer
#values
except ZeroDivisionError:
    print("invalid, divide by zero error")
else:
```

```
    # result is printed if there is no
#ZeroDivisionError
    print("result: ", result)
```

Creating Our Own Exceptions

As I mentioned in the introduction, there are some instances in which we want to create our own custom exceptions to make our code easier to debug, to check that our program behaves in the intended manner, and to have the ability to continue to use a try statement. We can create our own class to do this that extends *BaseException*, a built-in Python class from which all exceptions originate. Once we have setup the class for our exception, we can call it in our code. See the example below for the syntax of defining your own exception.

```
class InvalidPhoneException(Exception):
    def __init__(self, number):
        self.number = number
        self.message = "The phone number " +
str(self.number) + "was too long"

try:
    phone = int(input("What is your phone
number"))
```

```
    if len(phone) > 10:
        raise InvalidPhoneException(phone)
except InvalidPhoneException:
    print("Let's do something to handle the
exception")
```

In the example above, we defined an InvalidPhoneException. Notice, it is a subclass of the base class *Exception* which is passed inside parenthesis in the class definition. The example overrides the constructor to accept a phone number as an argument and to set the message of the exception. We use the *raise* keyword to trigger the exception if the phone number length is greater than 10 digits. We pass the phone number into the constructor of the exception because we defined this argument when we defined our own constructor, but we could also raise an exception without passing in an argument.

Breakpoints and IDLE Debugging

There is a wide variety of errors that will likely appear in your programs. Some of these errors will allow your program to run without crashing or raising an exception, but they will have an unintended effect on the function of your program. One error you will encounter (one of the most frequent for new coders) is a syntax error. A syntax error may be caused by something as simple as forgetting a colon after an if statement. The next error is a runtime error, which is produced by an error during program execution. Examples of runtime errors include infinite loops and invalid data type operations such as trying to subtract two strings.

The final main error is a semantic error. This occurs when your program runs without failing, but it doesn't function as intended. This is often the most difficult error to debug because the debug console doesn't output a line number where your code is erroneous since the interpreter thinks the code is running normally. Semantic errors can require extensive debugging and the use of breakpoints to trace the it. Often, the best way to debug these errors is to follow the execution of your program step by step to isolate the function or expression causing the unintended output.

In summary, here is a list of the main error types:

1. Syntax Error: invalid code statement or structure, such as omitting a needed symbol or using a construct not available in Python. A common syntax error occurs when code isn't indented inside a structure or some other invalid indentation.
2. Runtime Error: output by the system if something goes wrong during program execution. The interpreter

often outputs helpful debugging information such as the line number of the error.

3. Semantic Error: program executes without crashing, but doesn't work as intended. For example, a function may be expected to return a string, but it instead returns a floating-point value.

Using Print Statements

One way to debug a semantic error is with the use of print statements to follow the execution of your program and the value of variables at various points. Outputting the values of your program enables you to identify the point in which the code is not working as intended or determine the point at which it's crashing if it is causing a runtime error.

```
# the code below will not run
# assume get_user is a valid function

# retrieves profile with a username
def get_profile(username=""):
    # assume get_user is a valid function
    # user should be a dictionary with an id,
#name, grade, and school name
    user = get_user(username)
    print('debug: ' + user['grade']) # debug
#statement 1
```

```
    if user['grade'] > 9:
        print('debug: high school')  # debug
#statement 2
        user['high_school'] = True
    return user

# assume johnny05 is a 9th grade student
# gets a dictionary with the user profile
profile = get_profile(username='johnny05')

# outputs False when really it should output
#True since the student
# is in 9th grade. What went wrong??? Semantic
#error
print(profile['high_school'])
```

The example above is used to demonstrate a very simple debugging situation. Assume the program above runs, but it outputs false for the user's high school status when the user expects it to output true. Where did the program fail? It may be easy for you to recognize that it failed at the if statement. The condition should be changed to >= instead of >, but if this was a more complicated bug, how would you go about identifying it? That's why there are two print statements temporarily added to the code for debugging. They allow us to check the value of the user dictionary at various points and determine whether the if statement executed. At debug statement one, if the grade output was a value not equal to 9 and we expected the value to be 9, we then know that the failure originated in the *get_user* function and we should shift our debugging focus. If 9 is output as expected, but then our second debug statement isn't output, we would know that the if statement condition returned *False* when it should return *True*. At that point, we could read through our if statement and quickly determine that the error occurred due to implementing the incorrect comparison operator.

Breakpoints

We've seen how useful it can be to use print statements to trace program errors, but sometimes our errors are too complex to use print statements or we need to trace the function of a program line by line. Breakpoints are a debugging tool that pause our program at the line that they are set to display the value of runtime variables and allow us to trace program execution line by line. To set a breakpoint, you simply right click on the line and then select the "set breakpoint" menu option. The line will be highlighted, or it will have a small marker next to it. To get rid of a breakpoint, you can simply right click on it and select "clear breakpoint".

Let's examine a quick example in which we set a breakpoint in a program to see how it functions. Here is an example program you may quickly copy:

```
def even_message(number = 0):
    print(str(number) + " is even")


# breakpoint test to step through program
for i in range(1, 10):
    even = i%2
    if even == 0:
        even_message(number = i)
        print("That means it is divisible by 2")
```

In our example program, let's set a breakpoint at the assignment of the variable *even* and another at the print statement inside the for loop. Remember, right click on the line to set a breakpoint as seen in the next screenshot.

```
# breakpoint test to step through program
for i in range(1, 10):
    even = i%2
    if even == 0:
                              is even")
```

Cut
Copy
Paste
Set Breakpoint
Clear Breakpoint

Now, let's begin the debugging process in IDLE. Normally, when you run a program, you select the menu option that says "run module". For our program to pause at the breakpoints and display a debug console, we must first turn debugging on in IDLE. Open the IDLE Python shell where your program is run (not the window where you are editing your code) and select debug -> Debugger. A debug control window should appear after the menu selection, and your Python console should contain a message denoting that debug mode is on. Now, transition back to your Python file where you are editing your code and run the module. The next screenshot displays the editor on the left side of the screen and the Python shell on the right side.

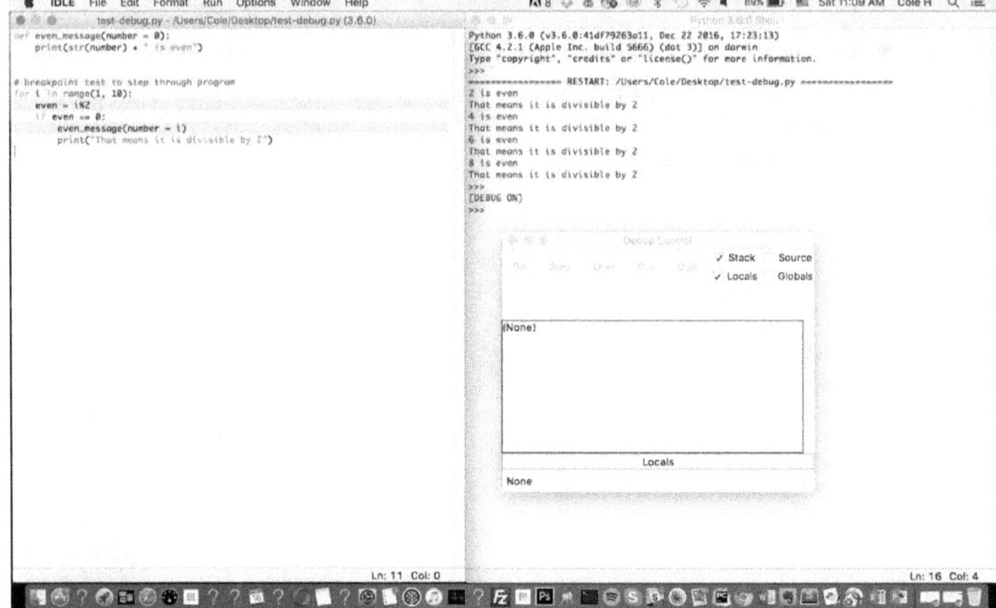

After running your code in debug mode, you will notice that it immediately pauses. The debug control window is populated with the local variables of the program and the debug trace. There are a few main controls at the top of the control window that allow us to work our way through the debug process. Here is the function of each control:

1. Go Button: Continues execution of program as normal until it hits the next breakpoint.
2. Step Button: Goes to the next line of the program. If the next line is a function call, it will go to the lines of code inside the function and walk through each line.
3. Over Button: Goes to the next line of a program when there is a function call instead of going to the code inside the called function.

4. Quit Button: Stops execution of the program and terminates the debugging process.

The locals window displays the items in the main namespace of the app. The output window above displays the line of the program that the debugger is at. Try pressing the *go* button. You will notice the program immediately skips to the first break point in our program, *even_message* is added to the locals, and *i* is added to the locals. This happens because this breakpoint occurs after the initialization of *i* and at the initialization of *even_message*. If you click the Step button, the debugger goes to the next line of our program. You will notice that the value of *even* in the locals area changes to one which is the value returned from the assignment expression.

If you click the *step* button at a function, the debugger will go to the code within that function. Click the *go* button until you get to the breakpoint at the line where the *even_message* function is called and then click the *step* button. The debugger will take you to the first line inside the function, in this case a print statement. If you click the step button again, it will go into the implementation of the print function. Since we are not concerned with tracing the implementation of the print function, click the *out* button to return to the next line of our program and exit the function traces. In the next screenshot, you can see how the out button returned to the top of the stack and shifted to the next line in our program.

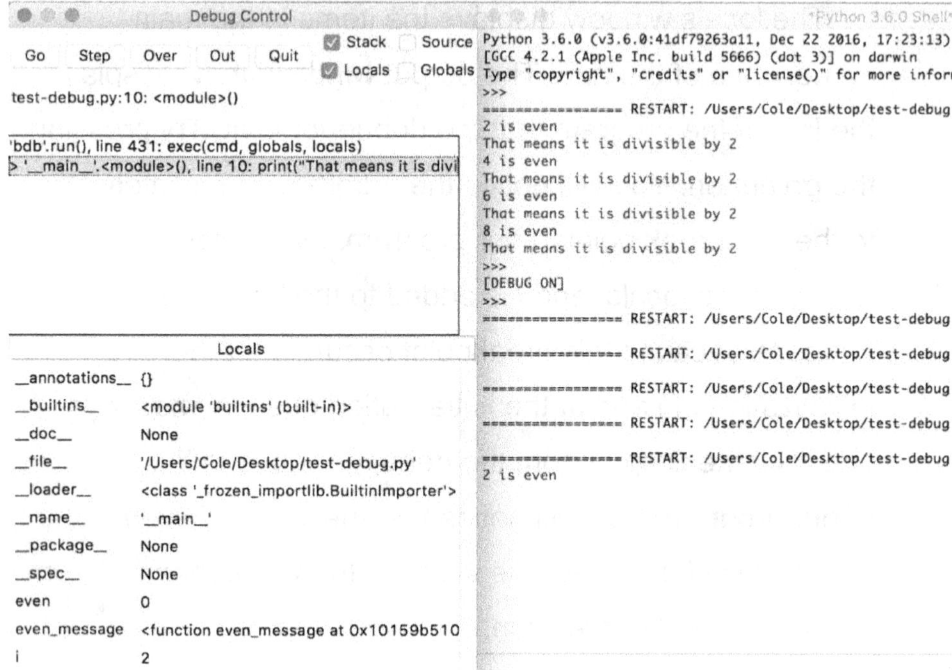

As you continue to experiment with the debug controls throughout the remainder of the program execution, notice how the variables *i* and *even* change with each loop iteration. Although this is a simple program, the debugger is a powerful tool because it allows us to follow the execution of our program and find the exact point in which it's failing or returning an unexpected result.

Conclusion:

Only those who don't code never need to debug. It's an essential part of developing programs, especially as they increase in complexity and function. To make the debug process as enjoyable as possible, make sure you are comfortable with the basic debugging tools available through IDLE. They demystify the execution of your program and give you an inside view on what is occurring. It's easier to debug a program when it is implemented in a friendly to read format from the beginning, meaning it's efficiently structured, divided into functions, commented, and easy to follow. Writing clean, friendly, and efficient code from the start will give you an upper hand in the debugging process. In messy programs, some coders end up scrapping entire sections of the program where a bug has occurred and starting from scratch. Commenting is such an essential component of this process because it allows you or other programmers to understand the implementation of your program, and it helps you avoid errors.

Ch. 8 Modules and Program Structure

Program Design and Modulation

You've seen most of the basic building blocks of Python programming from data types to control structures to functions. In our previous programs, all the Python code we have written has been placed and run in a single file. While this practice is acceptable for very small programs, it's not practical for larger and more complex ones. In building more complex programs, there is more than just the file structure we need to be concerned with. We must carefully consider the design of our code such as the naming of functions, structure of functions, error handling, and the efficiency of algorithms. In this chapter, we will examine some basic program design principles that will help make a larger project a more manageable one.

Program design is quite an extensive topic and in large teams at companies such as Facebook, there are software architects who are dedicated to this role. A software architect's job is to make high-level program design choices, set technical standards, and determine the libraries or tools the program will implement. While several books focus solely on this topic, we are going to look at a surface level overview for a beginner that is new to Python. First, I would like to point out that the purpose of careful program design is to ensure our code is easy to debug, easy to follow in the future, efficient, and collaborative. What I mean by collaborative is that you want another programmer to be able to read your code, figure out what it is doing, and contribute. Often, programmers need to access or make changes to code they wrote years, months, weeks, or even days earlier. With an easy to follow and optimal design structure, they should be able to quickly recognize how their program functions to begin making changes. In a poorly designed program, the programmer may not be able to follow the code implementation, and he or she is sometimes better off writing a new program from scratch.

Modules

You may not realize it, but we've been using modules all along. The file where you write your Python code is considered one. In simplest terms, a module is a Python file containing code such as control structures, functions, or classes. Modules allow us to separate our code into different components, and we can access code from each of the components. For example, there could be a module we have with a single class inside or a module of similarly grouped functions. We can access classes and functions of modules by importing them and referencing their namespace. Here is an example of using the *math* module that is built into Python:

```
import math
# using a function inside the math module
result = math.factorial(5)
print(result)
```

In the code above, *factorial* is a function that is part of the *math* module namespace. In order to implement it, we use the *import* statement followed by the module name. By importing the entire module, we can access to all properties of the math library. If you only wanted to import a limited number of functions from the math module, you could do the following:

```
from math import factorial, cos

# since we import the functions from the
#namespace, we don’t need the module name
# before calling the functions
r1 = factorial(3)
r2 = cos(0)
```

In the example above, notice we can call the *factorial* and *cos* functions without prefixing the calls with the *math* module name. This is because we import those specific functions into our own module namespace. When we import just the math module, we are referencing the math namespace and must prefix the function calls with the module name.

Overview of Module Structure

For a high-level overview of how our code may be divided into various modules, let's imagine we want to build a very simple weather program in Python that allows the user to type a city name in the console so he or she can retrieve info such as the temperature, wind speed, forecast, and elevation. Although the functionality of this program is straightforward, there is a plethora of components to handle ranging from outputting instructions to the user to retrieving real time weather data from a source such as openweathermap.org. One way to organize this program is to divide it into three main modules: a *main* module, a *weather* module, and an *api* module. The *main* module is responsible for handling user interaction and for starting our program. The *weather* module contains all the functions that retrieve needed data such as the forecast and temperature and return it in the appropriate format. The *api* module is responsible for handling http requests and interacting with

OpenWeatherMap's application programming interface (API). Here's a diagram of the basic structure:

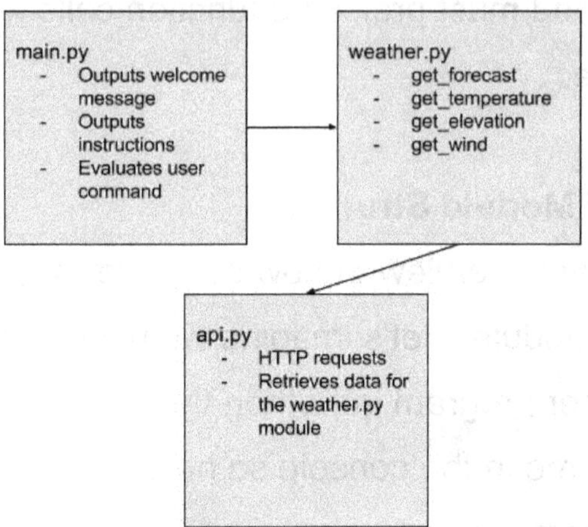

Creating Our Own Modules

Now that we've examined why modules are useful and have drafted a possible program structure, let's try to write our own simple program with modules. We are going to write a tic-tac-toe game with the use of modules to make our code more human readable. Here is the basic program structure:

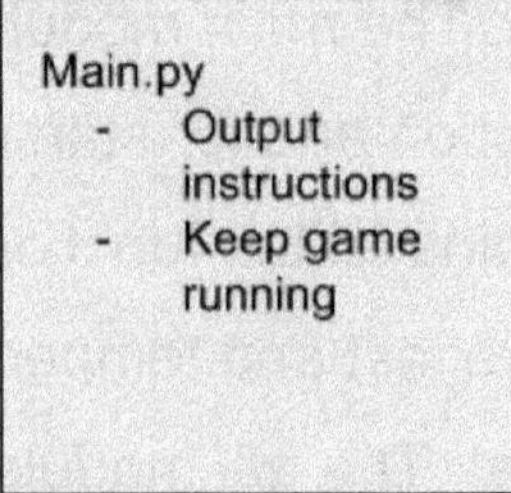

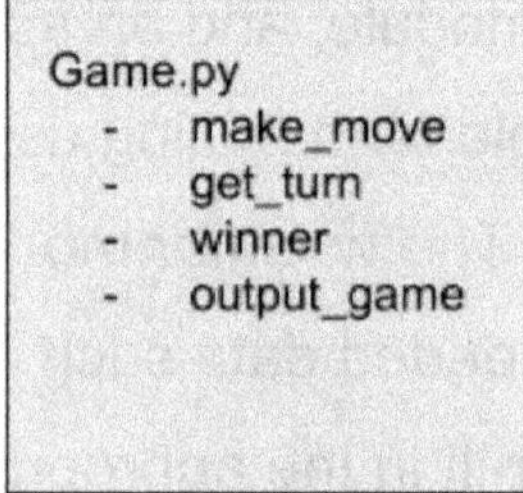

Our program is going to be divided into three different modules - *main.py*, *game.py*, and *player.py*. The *main* module is the Python file that will be run when playing our game, and it will import the other modules. The *game* module will have all the different game functions we need inside of a game class. This game class will be used to manage the board, player moves, the winner, and the next player move. The *player* module will contain a class that contains attributes and functions for a player such as the symbol that represents them in a game (an "X" or an "O"). Let's first examine the *player* module, see the screenshot below.

```
player.py - /Users/Cole/Desktop/tic-tac/player.py (3.6.0)
class Player:
    def __init__(self, username):
        self.username = username

    def set_symbol(self, s):
        self.symbol = s

    def get_symbol(self):
        return self.symbol
```

The *Player* class contains a constructor, a setter method, and an accessor method. We place it in a distinct module to make our program manageable and to separate program functionality. Using a player class of which we can instantiate objects is a more intuitive way of managing data in our program than using a structure like a dictionary, and it enables us to add methods and attributes. Let's examine the next file, *game.py*.

```
# game.py
import player


class Game:
    turn = 0

    def __init__(self):
        self.board = [["-", "-", "-"],
                      ["-", "-", "-"],
                      ["-", "-", "-"]]
        self.turn_count = 0




    def output_board(self):
        for row in self.board:
            row_string = ""
            for item in row:
                row_string += str(item) + " "
            print(row_string)

    def drop(self, row=0, col=0, player=""):
```

```
        self.board[row][col] = player

    def check_winner(self):
        for row in self.board:
            count = 0
            for index, item in enumerate(row):
                if (item == row[index-1] and
                   item != "-":)
                    count += 1
            print(count)

    def diagonal_check(self):
        count = 0
        for index, row in enumerate(self.board):
            if self.board[index][index] ==
               self.board[index+1][index+1]:
                count += 1
                if count == 2:
                    self.output_board()
                    break
    def make_move(self, row=0, col=0):
        self.board[row][col] =
self.turn.get_symbol()

        return self.board
```

```
def set_player1(self, username):
    self.player1 = player.Player(userna
    me=username)
    self.player1.set_symbol("x")

def set_player2(self, username):
    self.player2 = player.Player(username
    =username)
    self.player2.set_symbol("o")

def get_turn(self):
    if self.turn_count == 0:
        self.turn_count += 1
        turn = self.player1
        self.turn = self.player2
        return turn
    elif self.turn == self.player1:
        self.turn = self.player2
        return self.player2
    elif self.turn == self.player2:
        self.turn = self.player1
        return self.player1
```

The *game.py* file contains a game class that we use to manage a tic-tac-toe session. This module contains all the actions of the game, but it doesn't interact with the user to take choices for options such as the next move they would like to make. That functionality is reserved for our main module. In the constructor of the *Game* class, a blank three by three board is generated, and the number of turns that have occurred is set to zero. The *set_player* function allows us to assign player objects to the current game. The *output_board* function takes the multidimensional board list, formats it, and prints it out in the console. Notice that all the content of this module is exclusively focused on game data and logic. We do not ask the player for moves, we do not welcome the user, and we do not loop the game to keep it going. Next, let's examine the *main* module.

```
# main.py
import game as g
import player

def welcome():
    print("--- Welcome to Tic Tac Toe ---")


def loop_game():
```

```
    welcome()
    player1 = input("Player 1, select a
               username:")
    player2 = input("Player 2, select a
               username:")

    game = g.Game()
    game.set_player1(player1)
    game.set_player2(player2)

    while True:
        move = input("(" +
                game.get_turn().username + ")" +
                " What is your move?")
        game.make_move(int(move.split(" ")[0]),
        int(move.split(" ")[1]))
        game.output_board()

loop_game()
```

The main module is where we interact with the user to start the tic-tac-toe game. Our *welcome* function outputs a message with instructions to the user. Why use a function instead of just typing in several print statements? Well, making it a function was an intentional design choice to group the statements according to their purpose and to make it simple to update the messages later. It's more intuitive to see the *welcome* function call than having several print statements in a row and trying to determine exactly what they do. The point is when you have several commands that perform a single action, make those commands into a function. It's easier to follow the execution of your programs in terms of function calls instead of having several statements in either one function or one module that all perform different actions. This is why program design is so crucial, you must understand how to modularize your code, represent data, and correctly use functions.

The Use of Functions

I cannot stress enough the importance of logically naming your functions and frequently utilizing them to improve your code. Functions should contain lines of code that perform a specific action, and they should especially be used when that action is needed more than once in your program. For example, if you have a program in which you need to send a result to a server several times throughout your code, you should use a function.

Even if you only needed to send the result one time in your program, you should still have that code in a function to group it according to its functionality and to make it more readable. If you have code that uses an http request to send data to a server and read the server response, the lines will likely appear trivial to you when you revisit your code if they are not in a function. On the other hand, if they are grouped in a function and you see a function call such as *send_server* in your code, you will almost immediately remember how the program behaves. This exemplifies the importance of code design in the debugging process. Well-designed code allows you to follow the execution of a program and trace difficult errors.

Conclusion

Program design is an essential skill as a programmer. Don't feel overwhelmed. The task can be a bit intimidating considering there are software architects who essentially make a career out of maintaining and structuring the design of applications. It's something you will naturally get better at as you build more complex programs, work in teams, and receive feedback regarding your code. Also, there are some paradigms and standards in place, but the design structure is rather arbitrary – each programmer likely has different ideas concerning how a program should be structured. A general rule of thumb is you shouldn't be copying and pasting code. This means the code should be a function. You should make defined actions into a single function and place classes in their own module or sets of functions that exist for a similar purpose.

Ch. 9 Libraries and Dependency Management

Expanding Functionality with Libraries and Pip

Improving the functionality and complexity of our programs entails more than dividing code into modules. More complex programs perform tasks such as making http requests, displaying a graphical user interface (GUI), parsing data, visual processing, or scraping data from the web. These programs can quickly become thousands, hundreds of thousands, or even millions of lines codes depending on how advanced the end product is. Many of these functions such as making http requests are commonly used by many programmers. Libraries exist so we don't have to reinvent the wheel. If you need to scrape data from the web, why not save the time and use a library? Well, there are, of course, exceptions as to when you may not want to use a library such as building your own to understand the implementation or developing one with proprietary information.

Generally, our programs perform such a wide array of tasks that libraries are vital to being able to rather rapidly produce an end product. They are commonly used in applications and many are open source projects worked on by programmers around the world and websites such as

Github. The collaboration of programmers has provided the community of Python developers with a variety of libraries that make the language as powerful as it is to rapidly develop applications for different uses such as performing facial recognition, developing APIs, and web scrapping. To keep track of the libraries used in a program, we need a dependency management system like Pip. It is a default tool that is installed with Python, and it allows us to quickly integrate libraries into our applications. Without tools such as libraries and a dependency management system, programmers today wouldn't be able to rapidly prototype, collaborate in the same manner, nor could they deploy software quickly.

What is a library?

A library is packaged code that can be imported into a program so that its classes, attributes, or functions can be used. It's like a Lego piece that snaps on to our Lego structure (representative of our program) and adds functionality. Libraries save programmers time by allowing them to use the classes, modules, and other structures previously created and tested. This frequently keeps programmers from having to write similar code from scratch. Although some companies may charge for libraries, they are usually open source projects that are constantly being improved by programmers around the world. You may not

realize it, but we've already worked with libraries. We've used the Python Standard Library, a collection of built-in modules that provide the Python language with the ability to access system functions such as file handling.
Some of the functions of the standard library are highly specific to Python such as printing a stack trace while others are specifically oriented towards operating system functionality. Earlier in this book, we used the *math* module in an example program. We could import *math* at the top of our Python file and begin using it without any extra setup. That occurred because the *math* module is automatically built into the Python Standard Library. There are also objects from the library (functions and exceptions) that are in the Python Standard Library, but can be used without an import statement.

What is Pip?

In the context of business, a project manager or director is responsible for placing the people he or she needs on the team and ensuring that the group completes the task or goal at hand. Pip is like the project manager of libraries. It's a package manager included with Python that can retrieve dependencies, update them, or remove them so that we can simply import them into our programs. To see the current Pip installation, open a shell (Terminal on Mac), type *pip --version*, and press enter. See the screenshot below.

```
[Cole-Hersowitzs-MacBook-Pro:~ Cole$ pip --version                    ]
pip 9.0.1 from /Library/Frameworks/Python.framework/Versions/3.6/lib/python3.
6/site-packages (python 3.6)
Cole-Hersowitzs-MacBook-Pro:~ Cole$
```

Notice how the Pip version (9.0.1 in this case) was output on the next line of the terminal. To add a package (what we call a library in Python) with Pip, you type the following command in a terminal window, not the Python shell:

```
pip install package_name
```

The *package_name* needs to be replaced with the package you intend to install. After pressing enter, it will immediately begin to download, and it will be available in your Python programs upon successful installation. Unless we use a virtual environment, Pip will install dependencies system wide. This means that if we install a package with Pip, it will be available to all the Python projects that are using the same version. If you wanted a package to only be available to a project, you would need to use a semi-isolated Python environment called a virtual environment.

You may be wondering, how does Pip know what to download with just a package name? PyPI (the Python

Package Index) is a repository of software libraries that Pip interacts with. When you run the *pip install* command, it interacts with the PyPI server to initiate a download containing the specified package name. Each package has the same basic structure with a *setup.py* file to install the library after it is downloaded. A license text file such as an MIT License is usually included to describe how the library may be used.

Updating Pip

Sometimes you want to or need to update the version of Pip you are using. To do so, type the following in your terminal window:

```
pip install --upgrade pip
```

After pressing enter, the command should execute and the version should update upon a successful install.

Virtual Environments

When we open a terminal window and install a package with Pip, it's installed globally on our machine. While this setup will work, installing our dependencies globally isn't always an acceptable practice. What if we need to use Python 2.7 for a project? What if we need to use a different version of a dependency instead of the globally installed version? This is one reason we have *virtualenv,* a tool used to create semi-isolated Python environments on our machine. In large projects, it's often best to use a virtual environment to isolate all the packages and tools for a single project. Let's learn how to use *virtualenv* with a test project. Create a folder on your computer in a location that you can easily access such as your desktop. Open a terminal window, and *cd* into the directory (the folder) we just created. For example, if the folder I created is called test-pro and it was on my desktop, below is how I would access it:

```
[Cole-Hersowitzs-MacBook-Pro:~ Cole$ cd Desktop/test-proj
Cole-Hersowitzs-MacBook-Pro:test-proj Cole$
```

Now, let's install *virtualenv* on our machine with Pip. Type the following command and press enter:

```
pip install virtualenv
```

Since *virtualenv* has been installed, let's create an environment in our current project directory. We are going to be naming the environment *venv* (a common default convention), but you do have the ability to give it a different name:

```
[Cole-Hersowitzs-MacBook-Pro:test-proj Cole$ virtualenv venv
New python executable in venv/bin/python
Installing setuptools, pip, wheel...done.
Cole-Hersowitzs-MacBook-Pro:test-proj Cole$
```

To begin install dependencies in our virtual environment, we need to activate it. To do so, type the following command into your terminal with the name of your virtual environment (*venv* if you followed the instructions above):

```
source venv/bin/activate
```

After pressing the return key, your terminal will go to a new line and the name of your virtual environment will appear on the left in parenthesis. This means the environment is active. If you run the command *pip list*, you will notice that only the default dependencies for the virtual environment come up. Dependencies installed with Pip on your machine will not appear because this is a separate environment. To install dependencies within the virtual environment, you can now use *pip install* command as you would while normally adding a package because the virtual environment comes with Pip by default. As long as the environment is active, you will be installing dependencies to it instead of performing a system wide installation. For example, here is how I would install a commonly used package called *requests*:

```
[Cole-Hersowitzs-MacBook-Pro:test-proj Cole$ source venv/bin/activate
[(venv)Cole-Hersowitzs-MacBook-Pro:test-proj Cole$ pip install requests
Collecting requests
  Using cached requests-2.13.0-py2.py3-none-any.whl
Installing collected packages: requests
Successfully installed requests-2.13.0
(venv)Cole-Hersowitzs-MacBook-Pro:test-proj Cole$
```

If you proceed to run the *pip list* command, you will see the requests package appear in the list. For demo purposes, create a new file called *test.py* and save it in the project directory. Open the file, type the code below, and save the file.

```
import requests
r = requests.get('http://google.com/')
print(r.text)
```

With the virtual environment active in your shell, run *test.py* through the command line and observe the output below:

```
test-proj — -bash — 80×24
[(venv)Cole-Hersowitzs-MacBook-Pro:test-proj Cole$ python test.py
<!doctype html><html itemscope="" itemtype="http://schema.org/WebPage" lang="en"
><head><meta content="Search the world's information, including webpages, images
, videos and more. Google has many special features to help you find exactly wha
t you're looking for." name="description"><meta content="noodp" name="robots"><m
eta content="text/html; charset=UTF-8" http-equiv="Content-Type"><meta content="
/images/branding/googleg/1x/googleg_standard_color_128dp.png" itemprop="image"><
title>Google</title><script>(function(){window.google={kEI:'YZesWOaiKMz8jwPExbyQ
Dw',kEXPI:'1351903,1352241,1352382,1352623,1352690,1352701,1352808,3700328,37003
47,4029815,4032678,4038012,4041302,4043492,4045841,4048347,4062666,4065786,40678
60,4071842,4072773,4073405,4073412,4073655,4073728,4073958,4076096,4076999,40784
30,4078438,4079105,4079894,4081039,4081164,4082441,4082665,4083046,4083476,40854
12,4085682,4086011,4086074,4086699,4088341,4089003,4089118,4089183,4090352,40905
50,4090657,4090806,4090894,4092182,4092220,4092228,4092309,4092475,4092479,40928
97,4092934,4093498,4093948,4094251,4094544,4094768,4095381,4095907,4095999,40963
23,4096742,4096823,4096939,4097082,4097123,4097153,4097628,4097655,4097866,40979
22,4097929,4098733,4098740,4098752,4099337,4099359,8300272,8507381,8507860,85086
06,8508623,8509871,10200083,10202205,10202231,16200026',authuser:0,kscs:'c9c918f
0_24'};google.kHL='en';})();(function(){google.lc=[];google.li=0;google.getEI=fu
nction(a){for(var b;a&&(!a.getAttribute||!(b=a.getAttribute("eid")));)a=a.parent
Node;return b||google.kEI};google.getLEI=function(a){for(var b=null;a&&(!a.getAt
tribute||!(b=a.getAttribute("leid")));)a=a.parentNode;return b};google.https=fun
ction(){return"https:"==window.location.protocol};google.ml=function(){return nu
ll};google.wl=function(a,b){try{google.ml(Error(a),!1,b)}catch(c){}};google.time
```

Using the *requests* library (which we previously installed), this simple program retrieved the HTML and JavaScript code from the Google homepage. Notice how by using the *requests* package to make the http request, this program was only a few lines long, but there is a plethora of code contained in the package that is making this program function.

Exiting the Environment

How do you exit a virtual environment? Type the command below and your terminal will return to your regular system shell:

```
deactivate
```

Using a Particular Python Version

Sometimes, you want to create a virtual environment that uses a specific version of Python. For example, you may be contributing to an older program that is written in Python 2.7. If you ever need a virtual environment with a particular Python version, type the command below.

```
virtualenv -p path_to_Python venv
```

The value *path_to_Python* should be the file path to the version of Python on your machine you want to use. If you are using a Mac, the path may be something like

/Library/Frameworks/Python.framework/Versions/3.6/bin/Python3.

Conclusion

Even though we only used the *requests* package in a short program, trust the idea that libraries are important. Through your own development experiences in any programming language, you will see how they are pivotal in enabling you to rapidly build an application. You should now be familiar with the dependency manager Pip, and you should have some appreciation for how easy the Python Package Index makes it to quickly install dependencies. Remember to utilize virtual environments if needed for your Python projects. It helps you organize your dependencies, choose a particular Python version, and isolate your project. This is especially important when you start working on several diverse Python projects that each contain their own dependencies.

Ch. 10 Basic Networking

Making HTTP Requests

The internet has transformed the interaction of data, ideas, knowledge, and media. In Python programs, you often want the ability to interact with servers and access information from various databases or websites. HTTP (Hypertext Transfer Protocol) is the foundation of communication across the web. When you enter a web URL (uniform resource locator) in a browser, an http request is sent to fetch the web page you would like to load. While requesting information from a web URL is useful in a browser, it isn't exactly as useful when we are programming in Python. For example, if we make an HTTP request to the page showing trending topics on Reddit , the response received from the request is the actual web page code, meaning there is a bunch of html, JavaScript, and other nonsense we don't need. What if we just want the data from the page such as the titles of trending topics and the number of up votes?

Technically we can extract the data from the web page code in a process known as web scraping, but the preferred method of obtaining this data would be to use an API (application programming interface). They are available for different services including Facebook, Google, and Reddit. The advantage in interacting with an API is that they follow design standards in which they are meant to interact with programs. They are like the web browser for our Python programs. Although an entire book could be written solely on this topic, we are going to explore the basics of making HTTP requests by examining a simple Python program that interacts with Reddit.

REST

Representational State Transfer (REST) is a web architecture for a web service that uses HTTP for communication. A RESTful API is organized into components that are accessible with various HTTP methods. For example, if an API endpoint had a URL followed by '/users', *users* would be considered a component. An endpoint is some API URL that we can interact with. A REST server retrieves the components and returns it to the client. JSON is a common data format that is returned from the server. It can also be sent in requests. Let's examine the basic HTTP methods so we can better understand RESTful web systems.

Method	Description
GET	Retrieves a resource (ex. Fetching a web page)

POST	Updates existent resource or creates a new one (ex. Adding/Updating a comment)
PUT	Creates a new resource (ex. Posting a picture to a feed)
DELETE	Remove a resource (ex. Deleting an email or post)
OPTIONS	Retrieves supported operations (Returns valid methods such as GET or POST)

After a request is sent using one of the above methods, a status code is sent back from the server. The status code allows us to determine if the request was successful or if it failed. Have you ever seen a 404 error? That is an example of an http response code. Here are some common status codes:

Status Code	**Description**
200	Request Successful
400	Bad Request
403	Forbidden

404	Not Found
500	Internal Server Error

OAuth

There are different means of securing an API so that they are only accessible to developers or applications that are authorized to use them. For example, there is an HTTP Basic Authentication protocol, Digest Authentication protocol, OAuth 1, OAuth 2, and others. For the purposes of interacting with the Reddit API, we are just going to touch on some of the surface level details of OAuth 2. This protocol allows us to request an access token that we can then use to request a protected resource from the API. Here is a basic overview of how it works:

1. The client (the application that wants to access the user's account) requests authorization to access resources.
2. An authorization grant is returned if the request is properly authorized.
3. The authorization grant is sent to the API and an access token is issued if the authorization grant is valid and the client identity is authenticated.
4. The access token is sent with requests to API resources for authentication.

Getting Started with the Reddit API

In order for us to use oauth to access Reddit's API, we must register our application with the service. First, you need to sign up for an account with Reddit or login to an existing account. Next, go to the apps tab in Reddit account preferences (https://www.reddit.com/prefs/apps/).

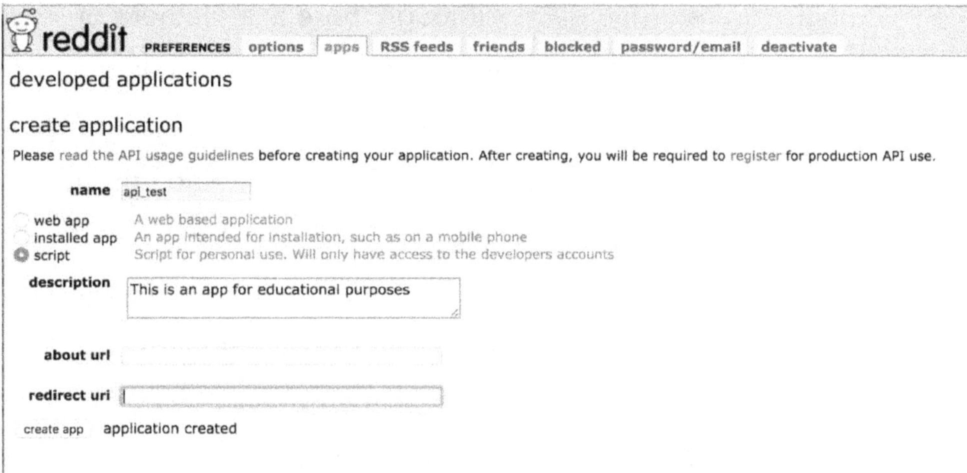

Create an application by providing a name, brief description, and redirect URL. If you don't have a website or particular location for the redirect url, you can use something such as a link to a Facebook page or google profile since this is just for simple educational purposes.

After creating the app, you will notice that it's saved on the apps tab and there is a secret key that is generated. We will need that information later, but for now it's time to test the API.

Testing Our Setup

Although some may view this as an optional step, it's generally beneficial to first use a REST client to test the requests we would like to make to the API. This process allows us to understand the structure of the API requests and to view the responses so we can decide on how to handle the returned data. Although there is a plethora of REST clients, one of my favorite tools is Postman (you can download it here: https://www.getpostman.com). Assuming you have installed Postman, let's quickly examine how to make a simple request to Reddit's API.

Once Postman is open, select GET as the request type and enter the following URL: http://api.reddit.com/r/space/new. The base url in this instance is http://api.reddit.com while the endpoint we are sending our request to is */r/animals/random*. Next, go to the authorization tab and select Oauth 2.0 from the dropdown menu. Entering the following data into the form:

1. Token Name - tok
2. Auth URL - https://www.reddit.com/api/v1/authorize
3. Access Token URL - https://www.reddit.com/api/v1/access_token
4. Client ID - series of characters that can be found on the app settings on Reddit under the application name
5. Client Secret - Located on the app settings on Reddit for the application you created earlier

Once you have entered the above fields on the form, select the button to request a new access token. We should now have the authentication we need to make requests to the API. Near our request URL, click the send button and observe the response in the window area below. The response should contain JSON data with subreddit listings as outlined in the Reddit documentation. Notice, the status code in the screenshot below is 200. If your request failed, look up the status code to help determine what may have gone wrong.

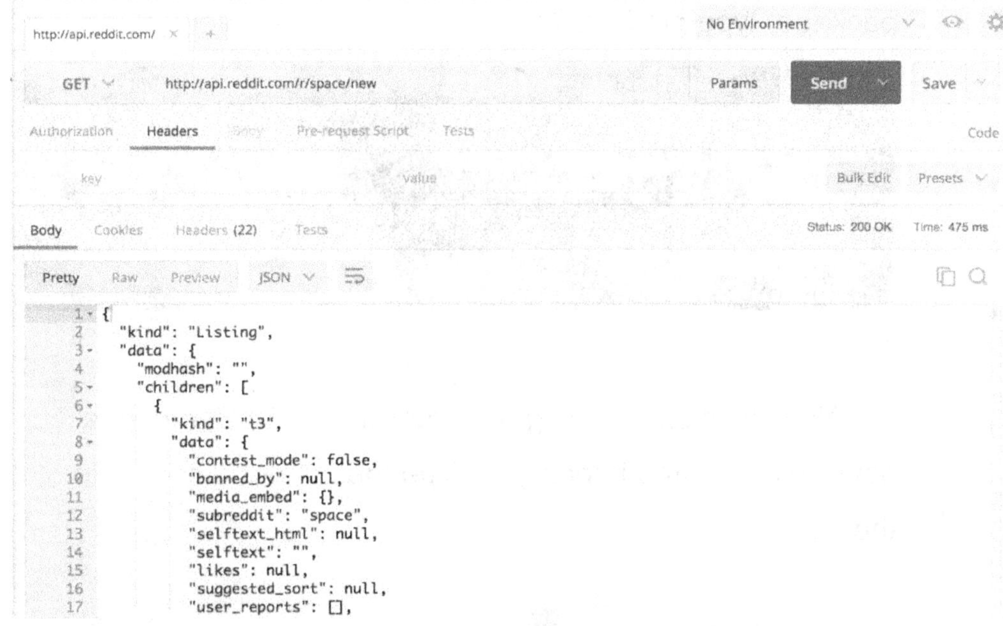

The Python Program

We are going to be writing a Python application that asks the user to enter a subreddit so that we can output a list containing the newest posts. To make HTTP requests, we are going to use a popular Python library called *requests* which has previously been mentioned. First, create a new directory (a folder) where you can store all the files for this project. Note the path of the newly created directory. Next, open a shell and change directory (use the cd command) into the directory you just created. To install the requests package, type *pip install requests* and press enter.

```
[Cole-Hersowitzs-MacBook-Pro:reddit-program Cole$ pip install requests
Collecting requests
  Using cached requests-2.13.0-py2.py3-none-any.whl
Installing collected packages: requests
Successfully installed requests-2.13.0
Cole-Hersowitzs-MacBook-Pro:reddit-program Cole$
```

Now, let's start coding our program. In IDLE, create a new file and name it *main.py*. Type the following code into the file:

```
import reddit


def ask_input():
```

```
    while True:
        user_in = input("Enter a subreddit: ")

        if len(user_in) > 0:
            return user_in


def welcome_message():
    print("Welcome to Reddit API program")
    print("Retrieve the newest posts from your
     favorite subreddit")

def print_posts(posts = []):

    for i, post in enumerate(posts):
        print("")
        print(str((i + 1)) + " " +
              post.get_title() + " (" +
              str(post.get_upvotes()) + "
              upvotes)")


def main():
    welcome_message()
```

```
    subreddit = ask_input()

    reddit_manager = reddit.RedditManager()
    posts = reddit_manager.get_listings(su
breddit=subedit)
    print_posts(posts=posts)


main()
```

The *main.py* file contains the primary application code, and it is separated into multiple functions for improved readability. There are three main high-level operations that need to be performed in this program. First, we must ask the user to enter a subreddit and validate this input. Next, we must retrieve the subreddit posts using the API. Lastly, the fetched posts need to be output to the console. The step of asking the user for a subreddit is encapsulated in its own function named *ask_input*. This function uses a loop to continue asking the user for a value, and it validates the value by checking that its length is at least one character. Once an inputted value has been successfully validated, the *ask_input* function returns this string.

The *RedditManager* is a class that is responsible for utilizing the API and making the responses into *Post* objects. The *get_listings* methods returns a list of *Post* objects, each one with a *get_title* method and a *get_upvotes* method. The *print_posts* function, which is also defined in this main module, is responsible for iterating through a list of *Post* objects and outputting the information in a neat format down in the console. In this case, we output a single line containing a number, title, and the number of up votes for each post. See the console output below.

```
Welcome to Reddit API program
Retrieve the newest posts from your favorite subreddit
Enter a subreddit name: space

1 NASA officials discuss Trump's push for first-term moon mission (1 upvotes)

2 Question: Can someone explain the Pulsar map (0 upvotes)

3 Weekly Space Hangout - Feb 24, 2017: 7 New Exoplanets Around TRAPPIST-1 and More! (2 up

4 What are some interesting medical / biological things that can happen in zero-gravity?
```

In IDLE, create a new file called *api.py*. This module will be responsible for handling the program's HTTP requests. It contains a class called *ApiManager* that is instantiated with a base URL, client id, and a secret key. A method called *get_access_token* is responsible for authorizing requests by sending a request to retrieve an access token that can later be used to retrieve data from endpoints.

The *get* method, which takes an endpoint as an argument, is responsible for calling the *get_access_token* method to retrieve a token, adding that token to a request as a parameter, and executing a GET request with the specified endpoint. This function then returns the JSON response data. The endpoint parameter should be the URL extension of the base URL. For example, the base URL for the Reddit API is http://api.reddit.com, and the extension passed in as a parameter may be a path such as */r/space/new*. Below is the code contained in the *api.py* file. Make sure you replace the username and password with the corresponding login information for your Reddit account at the *get_access_token* function call inside the *get* method definition.

```
import requests
import requests.auth
import uuid

class ApiManager:

    def __init__(self, base_url="",
                 client_id="", secret=""):
        self.base_url = base_url
        self.client_id = client_id
        self.secret = secret

    def get_access_token(self, token_url="",
        username="", password=""):
        client_auth = requests.auth.HTTP
```

```
    BasicAuth(self.client_id, self.secret)
    params = {"grant_type": "password",
    "username": username, "password":
     password}
    headers = {"User-Agent":
                uuid.uuid4().__str__()
    }
    resp = requests.post(token_url,
            auth=client_auth, data=params,
            headers=headers)

    return resp.json()['access_token']

def get(self, endpoint=""):
    tok = self.get_access_token(token_url=
        "https://www.reddit.com/api/v1/acc
         ess_token",
         username="ENTER_YOUR_USERNAME",
         password="ENTER_YOUR_PASSWORD")
    params = {"access_token": tok }

    response =requests.get(url=(
     self.base_url + endpoint),
     params=params)
    return response.json()
```

Create a new file called *reddit.py* in IDLE. This module will contain the *Post* class to represent Reddit results and the *RedditManager* class to handle the request of data from the Reddit API and the creation of *Post* objects with the response data. The constructor of the *RedditManager* class takes a base URL (http://api.reddit.com/), client id (found in the Reddit settings page), and a secret key (also found in the settings). The *get_listing* function accepts the name of a subreddit as an argument, and it calls the API manager to make a GET request with the constructed path. A response is stored from the GET request and iterated over to produce *Post* objects from the JSON data. The *Post* class has a constructor that accepts the title and the number of up votes as arguments. Since this is set upon object initialization, we can later call the *get_title* or *get_upvotes* methods to retrieve this data for each post.

```
import api


class Post:
    def __init__(self, title="", up_votes=0):
        self.title = title
        self.up_votes = up_votes
```

```
    def get_title(self):
        return self.title

    def get_upvotes(self):
        return self.up_votes

class RedditManager:

    def __init__(self):
        self.api_manager = api.ApiManager(base
            _url="http://api.reddit.com",
            client_id="YOUR_CLIENT_ID",
          secret="YOUR_SECRET_KEY")

    def get_listings(self, subreddit):
        json_d = self.api_manager.get
        (endpoint="/r/" + subreddit + "/new")

        posts = []

        for item in json_d['data']['children']:
           post = Post(title=item['data']
            ['title'],
            up_votes=item['data']['ups']
```

```
        )
            posts.append(post)

    return posts
```

Once the *api.py*, *main.py*, and *reddit.py* files are created, you must run the main module to execute the program. The main module starts the program by calling the main function and initializing the needed objects such as a *RedditManager* object. This program doesn't only demonstrate the basics of making HTPP requests. It also implements some of the design principles discussed earlier in this book. There is a key component in this program that is missing – error handling. The program works perfectly fine when the server response is exactly what we expect, but it crashes if the server response is erroneous. As a result, this is far from a production ready program, but the point of this simple program was to expose you to the basics of networking, the *requests* package, and the implementation of more complex programs.

Conclusion

Due to the prevalence of the internet and our interconnected world, understanding networking is essential to developing useful applications in Python or other programming languages. HTTP is a communication protocol managed by the Internet Engineering Task Force and the Request for Comments (RFC) is a document published outlining the principal development standards of the Internet. You should now be familiar with the basics of HTTPS requests and the different methods such as GET and POST. Application Programming Interfaces (APIs) are available for most large programs as a means of receiving data from or sending data to servers. We explored the basics of the Reddit API through an example application. The ability to use APIs and networking libraries such as *requests* vastly expands your ability to write more powerful and practical Python programs that leverage data from the web to solve a problem or accomplish a goal.

Ch. 11 Unit Testing
Another Crash Preventer

Your programs are beginning to increase in size and complexity, and sometimes, these programs crash. Often, you can use a debugger and other tools we've previously discussed in this book, but it's time to take it a step further. It's time to help you refrain from unintentionally breaking your programs and to help you write less buggy code. Unit testing is a level of software testing in which individual components such as function calls are evaluated to ensure they work as intended and contain the expected result. It helps us quickly identify errors with the simplest components of programs and ensure that code still functions as expected after substantial changes. Especially as a program increases in complexity, it's important for you to check that each individual unit functions as expected instead of just observing the result of the integrated program.

During the testing process, we need to write code in test cases that call code we would like to evaluate and check the output. The *unittest* framework is included in the Python Standard Library, and it allows us to setup these test cases. The time you invest in writing test cases will save time later in the development life cycle of an application by ensuring code works under a set of conditions, checking for basic errors, and ensuring changes do not break existing functionality. Since unit testing requires modular code, it is also a decent means of evaluating the design of your application, and it may cause you to make different design decisions.

Test Cases

A test case should be written in its own file and prefixed with a keyword such as *test* to differentiate it from your other program files. You can also place test cases in their own subdirectory to help organize your project. First, a test case must import the *unittest* library. A test class is created by extending the *TestCase* class and each test is added as a function inside. To access the functions or classes you have written and would like to test, you must also import these into the module. Here is the basic structure of a test case:

```
import unittest
from my_module import something
class TestCase(unittest.TestCase):

    def test_something(self):
        self.assertTrue(check a condition)
```

```
if __name__ == '__main__':
    unittest.main()
```

If you run the module, IDLE will output each test and show you whether they passed or failed. In this case, the *assertTrue* statement is the determining factor of the test passing. To add more tests to this case, additional functions can be defined below the example function. In a situation in which there are multiple test cases you would like to execute, a test suite may be used to aggregate tests to execute them at the same time. Although not an exhaustive list, results of a test may be checked with some of the following methods:

Method	Description
assertEqual(*a*, *b*)	Checks a equals b
assertNotEqual(a, b)	Checks a does not equal b
assertTrue(*a*)	Checks a is True
assertFalse(*a*)	Checks a is False
assertIsNone(a)	a is of type None

assertGreater(a, b)	Check a is greater than b
assertLess(a, b)	Check a is less than b
assertRaises(a)	Check than an exception (a) is raised

Let's Get Testing

To learn how to unit test, let's setup a simple test case for the *Post* class we created in the *api.py* file from the project last chapter. As a reminder, here is the code for the *Post* class:

```
class Post:
    def __init__(self, title="", up_votes=0):
        self.title = title
        self.up_votes = up_votes

    def get_title(self):
        return self.title

    def get_upvotes(self):
        return self.up_votes
```

In the project directory, create a new file called *test_reddit.py*. Then, write the following code to setup the test case:

```
import unittest
import reddit

class RedditTestCase(unittest.TestCase):

    def setUp(self):
        self.post = reddit.Post(title="wall
        street", up_votes=5)

    def test_get_upvotes(self):
        self.assertEqual(self.post.get_upvotes(),
        5)

    def test_get_title(self):
        self.assertEqual(self.post.get_title(),
        “wall street”)

if __name__=='__main__':
    unittest.main()
```

In the case above, we initialize a *Post* object in the setup method and store it in a variable called *post* that we can use throughout each test. Then, two tests in this case are executed, one to check the up votes of the post and another to check the title. If the values returned from each method call equal the values we expect, then the test passes. You should see something like the output below in the Python console when you run the *test_reddit.py* file:

```
..
----------------------------------------------------------------------
Ran 2 tests in 0.053s

OK
```

Let's intentionally make a test fail to see the result. Change one of the *assertEqual* function calls to *assertNotEqual* and run the module. In the case below, I added *the assertNotEqual* method to my *get_title* test, and the following was output:

```
F.
======================================================================
FAIL: test_get_title (__main__.RedditTestCase)
----------------------------------------------------------------------
Traceback (most recent call last):
  File "/Users/Cole/Desktop/reddit-program/test_reddit.py", line 13, in test_get
_title
    self.assertNotEqual(self.post.get_title(), "wall street")
AssertionError: 'wall street' == 'wall street'

----------------------------------------------------------------------
Ran 2 tests in 0.048s

FAILED (failures=1)
```

The console output provides a traceback to the error, shows us the value that was returned from the function calls, and tells us the number of tests run in a period of time along with the number of failures.

A test suite is a collection of test cases or other suites, and it allows us to aggregate tests. If there were multiple test cases in the *test_reddit.py*, a suite would offer finer control over the testing process by allowing us to exclude certain cases and set the test runner. For demo purposes, delete the block of code begin with the statement *if __name__* == and add a suite with the following code:

```
suite = unittest.TestLoader().loadTestsFromTe
stCase(RedditTestCase)

unittest.TextTestRunner(verbosity=5).run(suite)
```

Now, if you run the code, it should execute our test case like before. What's advantageous about this suite is that if we add more test cases, we can control which cases we would like to run. For example, if we want to run an additional case with this suite, we would simply pass the test case in as another argument of the *loadTestsFromTestCase* method call.

Skipping Test Cases

Sometimes, you want to skip tests because you know they repeatedly fail or you have stubbed a test and don't have any code inside. You may also want to skip a test if your program is running on an incompatible machine or a library version is unsupported. To skip, you pass use the *pass* keyword or a unit test decorator. Here are some basic decorators and their functions:

Decorator	Description
unittest.skip(*reason*)	Skips test unconditionally, reason should describe why
unittest.skipIf(condition, reason)	Skip a test if the condition is true
unittest.expectedFailure()	Mark as an expected failure; the failed test doesn't count as a failure

Decorators are written on the line above the function you would like to skip at the same indendation level as the declaration. Here is a decorator for the test_get_upvotes function call:

```
@unittest.skip("Skipping this")
def test_get_upvotes(self):
    self.assertTrue(self.post.get_upvotes(
    )==5)
```

Now, if you run the test module you will notice that the test is marked as skipped along with a message that should describe why it is being skipped. The output also notifies us that two tests were run, but of those tests, one of them was skipped. Okay, let's say I want to add a new test, but don't want to implement it yet. I could use the *pass* keyword as seen below.

```
def test_get_comments(self):
    pass
```

This test would automatically be marked as successful with the *pass* keyword. Now when you run the test module, it will output that three tests run within a time period.

Conclusion

Unit testing is an important component of any software development lifecycle to ensure that the parts of program work as intended. When multiple function calls and classes are integrated together, it becomes more difficult to find the true cause of certain bugs and to test the integrity of the program. To understand the importance of unit testing, let's compare it to learning calculus at school. When you are in the course, you study multiple topics such as the chain rule, and you are tested after learning a topic. Each math test evaluates whether you have mastered the topic or not. If you receive a bad grade, it indicates you should go back to review the material. If you pass all the previous math tests, then it is likely you will pass the final exam.

Unit testing software allows us to break down problems, check up on our progress, and try to prevent daunting errors. Sometimes, code may function perfectly fine, but then you refactor it, unknowingly breaking it in the process. Frequently running unit tests alerts you to these kinds of mistakes. There are entire books on testing. It can be quite a complex topic, but hopefully you are at least familiar with the basics of unit testing in Python, now that you've read this chapter.

Ch. 12 Development Tools
Git, PyCharm, and Documentation

IDLE has been a great integrated development environment up to this point in time, but as you improve your Python programming skills, you will quickly long for more advanced coding tools. It's like learning to ride a bike with training wheels, then learning to drive, and then wanting to drive a Lamborghini Aventador or a Bugatti Chiron. Although IDLE is a decent default program, there are more advanced IDEs such as PyCharm that offer better syntax highlighting, an improved UI, a file manager, a more powerful debugger, and other features. As you increase the size of your programs, you will also learn to appreciate version control systems such as Git. Completely broke your code? No problem, just revert to your last change with Git. Want to collaborate with other programmers? Well, Git makes this relatively straightforward. You can have each team member work on their own branch.

To be a self-reliant and effective programmer, it's important that you understand how to read documentation. There are so many classes and functions in the Python Standard Library, you can't possibly memorize all of them which is why we have documentation. Don't remember how to open a file? Well, look at the documentation. This skill is applicable to more than just the Python Standard Library – documentation exists for other programming languages, APIs, and tools. Remember the Reddit program? Well, you can look at the documentation for the Reddit API to view the different endpoints available along with the request parameters and responses.

IDE Upgrade – PyCharm

If you want the Rolls Royce of IDEs, you should download PyCharm, an environment developed by the company JetBrains. There is a lightweight community edition you can download for free here: https://www.jetbrains.com/pycharm/download/. PyCharm offers improved syntax highlighting, debugging tools, and project management features that are not available to us in IDLE.

As you can see in the next screenshot, a file directory tab enables you to quickly view the file structure of your project, you can rapidly create new Python files, and you can immediately access the Python console or terminal window at the bottom. As you start typing code, autocomplete enables you to access the various functions or classes of a module, saving you time from having to look up the exact structure of a function call.

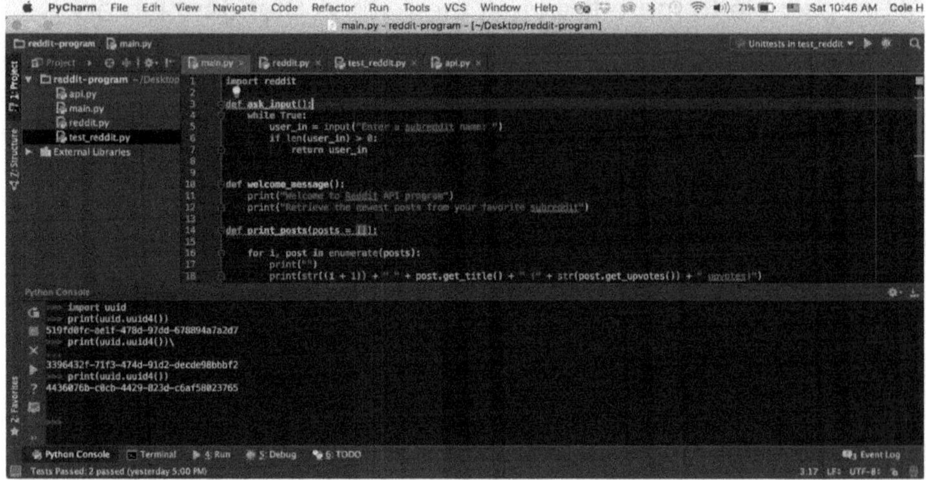

The preferences in IDLE enable you to manage which Python interpreter you are using for a project, and you can create virtual environments with the setup tool. You can also install dependencies with Pip through a UI in the preferences window. We can refactor code with PyCharm, and we can rename module files while updating the name elsewhere to avoid breaking the program. When writing large programs, you often begin to write code such as function, but may only layout the basic structure (a process called stubbing) or not finish it. With PyCharm, you can place the keyword *TODO* in a comment above a function and this will be tracked by PyCharm, appearing under the TODO tab so that you can quickly navigate back to this point in your program later and so that you remember to complete it. You can also leave a message in the *TODO* comment to remind you of the task that needs to be performed.

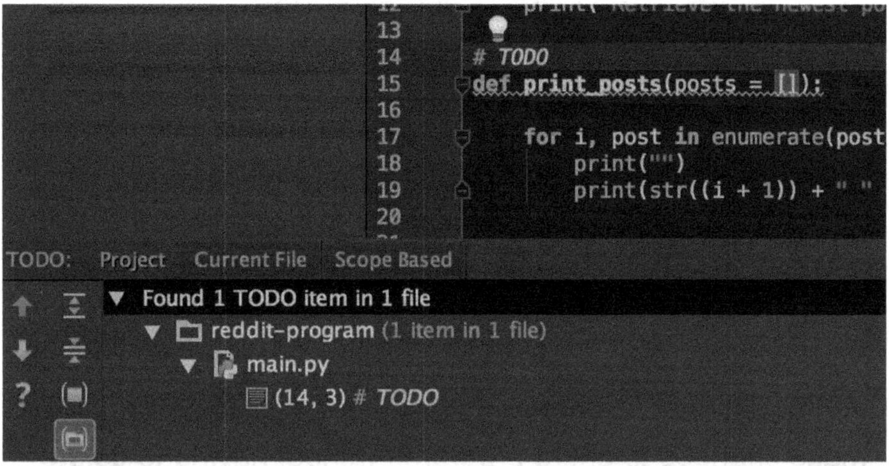

You can register version control in your project settings, view documentation, and view quick function definitions. There is a plethora of features I have not mentioned regarding PyCharm, but I recommend you download it, code with it, and explore its true power.

Version Control with Git

As your projects increase in size, you will frequently make errors that break once-functioning code. You may want to add a new feature to an application, or you may want to work with a project in a test environment instead of the production environment. If you truly want to build awesome software, you will work with a team of people. Version control can facilitate these different use cases. There are teams of hundreds of programmers at large companies all working on applications simultaneously. This type of collaboration is only feasible with a version control system (VCS), and Git is one of the most popular in the world. Git is a decentralized VCS, meaning copies of code are stored on each developer's machine while others systems such as Subversion are centralized in which developers use a single shared repository.

Good version control should allow you to facilitate continuous program changes, whether you are working alone, with a small group, or in a large team. It allows you to make changes to entire programs without having to delete code, and it gives you the freedom to try new features or programming practices. You can always fall back on an earlier version of the program if it doesn't function as intended.

GitHub

You may understand Git, but what is GitHub? Well, it's a widely popular repository hosting service which you can use to manage your projects. There are other services such as Bitbucket, but GitHub is home to a large community of over ten million developers, and it offers a dynamic platform for project collaboration. It's free to get an account, and they even offer a nifty student pack. The pack allows you to access software and programs such as Atom, Amazon Web Services, Digital Ocean, and Stripe. Currently, Namecheap offers a complimentary one year domain registration for *.me* TLDs with the student pack. Sign up for GitHub at https://github.com or get your student pack here: https://education.github.com/ pack/offers

First Git Repository

To learn about the basics of Git, let's create our first project on GitHub. Login to your account. From the top menu bar, click a button that says "New Repository". A repository (sometimes referred to as a repo) is a collection of files for your project. While creating a repository, you have the option to make it either public or private. If it's private, the repo will only be accessible to collaborators that you specifically grant access to. You also have the option to choose a license and to initialize it with a readme file. For demo purposes, let's say you want to upload your Python program that interacts with the Reddit API. Name the repository something logical such as *reddit-Python-demo* and make it private or remove the secret key from your program.

The next step is to install Git on your computer. This step is going to vary depending on the operating system you are using and the installation method you choose to use. If you are on Mac OSx Mavericks 10.9 or above, you can simply open a terminal window and type *git*. After running the command, it should prompt you to run an installation if it isn't already installed. If you are on Windows, Linux, or a different version of Mac OSx, you may also download an installation from the Git website: https://git-scm.com/downloads.

After installing Git, open a shell and cd (change directory) into the directory of the project you would like to manage with Git (in this case our Reddit API project). Once you are in the directory, initialize a local Git repository with the *git init* command. See the screenshot below and notice

```
reddit-program — -bash — 80×24
Cole-Hersowitzs-MacBook-Pro:reddit-program Cole$ ls
__pycache__     api.py          main.py         reddit.py       test_reddit.py
Cole-Hersowitzs-MacBook-Pro:reddit-program Cole$ git init
Initialized empty Git repository in /Users/Cole/Desktop/reddit-program/.git/
Cole-Hersowitzs-MacBook-Pro:reddit-program Cole$
```

how this occurs in the project directory.

After a local Git repository has been initialized, we need to add our remote GitHub repo. Go to your repository on GitHub, click the button that is labeled “clone or download”, and copy the remote URL featured in the drop-down menu. Then, go back to your shell in which you initialized the local repo and type the following command:

```
git remote add origin paste_your_url_here
```

After running the command, a new Git remote with the name origin will be available for us to use. First, we need to pull from the remote Git repo to retrieve the README file that was created upon its creation. Then, we can commit all our files and push them back to the remote. Run the following commands in the shell:

```
git pull origin master
git add -A
git commit -m "initial commit"
git push origin master
```

In the command prompt, there should be some output denoting the fact that the code was pushed to the repository. Now, go to the repository on GitHub and refresh the page. You should see all the code you pushed along with a commit history and branch information. Now that you've pushed your first repo to GitHub, let's further develop our understanding of the practical implementation of Git.

The Basics of Using Git

There are some basic concepts of Git that you should be familiar with to successfully utilize it. First, you must understand that a repository, as previously mentioned, is a collection of files including code, images, assets, and other project assets (such as a README markdown file). Another important feature of Git is branching which enables you to work on different versions of a project simultaneously. By default, repositories have a branch called *master*. When you branch off *master*, you are working with a snapshot or copy of *master* at that point of time in which the new branch was created. Generally, you want your *master* branch (often the production branch) to contain your latest stable version of the project code. You should use branches for developmental changes or features. After working on a branch, the code can then be merged back into *master* once it's proven to be stable or has met your standards.

To create a new local branch and use it, open the shell, cd into the project directory where you setup your repo, and type the following command:

```
git checkout -b dev
```

This creates a new branch off master and moves the HEAD (the current commit) to the branch. Type the command below, and notice how terminal outputs that we are on the *dev* branch after its execution.

```
git status
```

For the purpose of experimenting with branches, create a new file in the project directory on this branch and save it as *test.txt* (place some random text inside the file, it really doesn't matter). Now, let's commit our change and push it to this newest branch. Type the following commands:

```
git add -A
git commit -m "added a file for demo"
git push origin dev
```

The code should have been successfully pushed. Go back to the repo on your GitHub account and click on the branch button. You should see a new remote branch called dev in the list. If you click on it, you will see that your *test.txt* file is on that branch, but not on master.

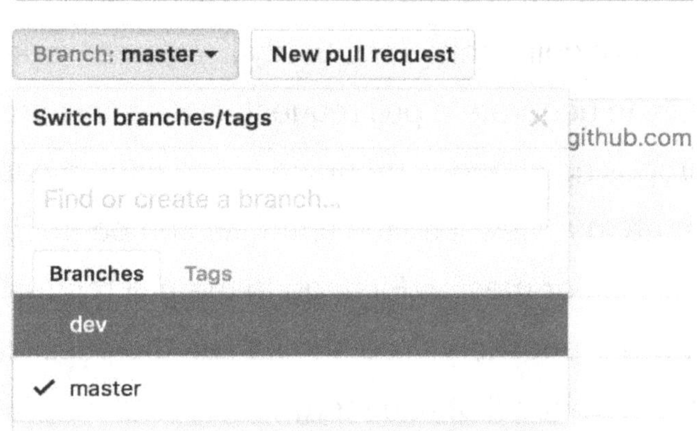

In the previous commands, we have been making commits (saved changes) and giving each one a message describing those changes. A commit message may briefly describe a new feature, bug fix, or update. Making a commit is like saving a document on Microsoft Word after making changes you want to ensure are not lost and leaving yourself a note in the process. Under the commits tab on GitHub, you can review each of your previous commits along with the messages for each and actual code changes. If you are working on a team, you can read through the commits of your team members and see exactly how they modified their code. Commits are important because they are descriptive of project changes and act as points that you can revert to if something goes wrong.

In this GitHub example, we now have two branches of code: one called *dev* and one called *master*. How do we merge *dev* back into *master* to incorporate the changes? One way of doing this, specifically if you are working on a team, is to generate a pull request. During this process, you are proposing changes be made to the code by asking someone to review it so the changes can be merged into their branch or *master*. First, go to the pull requests tab in the GitHub repository. You should see the possible commits and file changes that can merged.

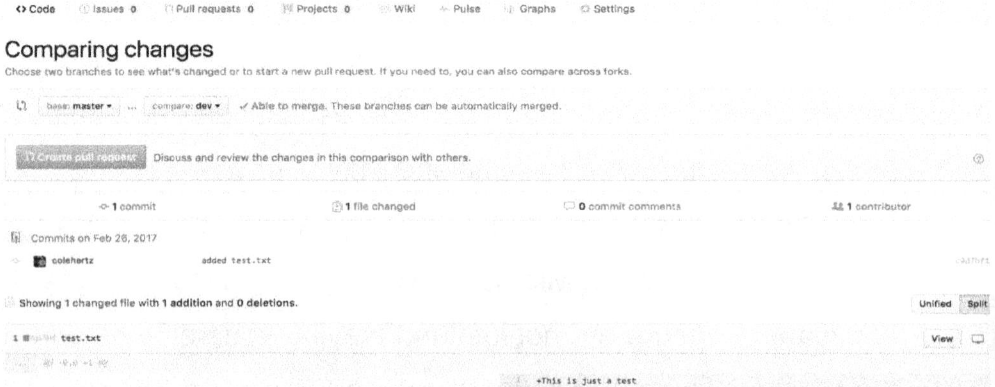

Commits from the comparison branch (*dev*) will be merged into the base (in this case *master*). Now, click the button to create a pull request and add a comment. In this case, you are the only collaborator on this repository. If you were working on a team, collaborators would be able to see the commits you would like to merge, and they would be able to comment on these changes. Assuming you would still like to go through with the code changes, click the *merge pull request* button and confirm the merge.

Go back to the code tab on GitHub and observe the contents of the *master* branch. You will notice that the test file you previously created on the *dev* branch has been merged into *master*, and the merge shows up in the repo commit history. Pull requests are essential when working in a team environment. Although, in the example above which contains no collaborators on the repo, you could also switch to the master branch, run the merge command, and then push your changes to the remote repo after the local merge. See the screenshot below to merge locally.

```
reddit-program — -bash — 80×24
[Cole-Hersowitzs-MacBook-Pro:reddit-program Cole$ git checkout master
Switched to branch 'master'
[Cole-Hersowitzs-MacBook-Pro:reddit-program Cole$ git merge dev
Updating 39227f3..aa800ac
Fast-forward
 test.txt | 2 +-
 1 file changed, 1 insertion(+), 1 deletion(-)
Cole-Hersowitzs-MacBook-Pro:reddit-program Cole$
```

We have just scratched the surface regarding how Git can be utilized for your projects. Here is a reference table of some Git commands you may find useful:

command	Description
git init	Initialize an empty git repository
git clone *url*	Make a copy of a git repo at a url
git status	List file changes and those you still need to commit
git fetch origin	Fetch the latest history and changes from the origin remote
git branch -d *branch*	Delete a branch (branch = the branch name to remove)
git log	View commit history

Documentation

The task of a programmer is not to simply recall information, but rather to design, develop, and maintain software programs. If programming was about memorization, it would be a burdensome task to remember the exact syntax of each language, the function calls, libraries, available classes, and other language features. Instead, there is documentation for programming languages and libraries. It's like a hybrid between a dictionary for programming languages and an instruction manual. The most important documentation you should first familiarize yourself with is the Python docs (https://docs.Python.org/3/). They contain tutorials, information on modules, language reference, and information on the Python Standard Library.

The documentation for the Python Standard Library is your cheat sheet. It tells you about the various data types, exceptions, file access methods, internet protocols, and more. What if we are working with strings and we want to know which methods are available through the Python Standard Library? Well, we could check the documentation and read about the various methods including the function of each, parameters, and return types. Here is a screenshot of part of the Python documentation:

4.7.1. String Methods

Strings implement all of the common sequence operations, along with the additional methods described below.

Strings also support two styles of string formatting, one providing a large degree of flexibility and customization (see `str.form` String Syntax and Custom String Formatting) and the other based on C `printf` style formatting that handles a narrower range of slightly harder to use correctly, but is often faster for the cases it can handle (printf-style String Formatting).

The Text Processing Services section of the standard library covers a number of other modules that provide various text re (including regular expression support in the `re` module).

`str.`**`capitalize`**`()`
Return a copy of the string with its first character capitalized and the rest lowercased.

`str.`**`casefold`**`()`
Return a casefolded copy of the string. Casefolded strings may be used for caseless matching.

Casefolding is similar to lowercasing but more aggressive because it is intended to remove all case distinctions in a string. the German lowercase letter `'ß'` is equivalent to `"ss"`. Since it is already lowercase, `lower()` would do nothing to `'ß'`; converts it to `"ss"`.

The casefolding algorithm is described in section 3.13 of the Unicode Standard.

New in version 3.3.

`str.`**`center`**`(`*width*`[, `*fillchar*`])`
Return centered in a string of length *width*. Padding is done using the specified *fillchar* (default is an ASCII space). The oriç returned if *width* is less than or equal to `len(s)`.

`str.`**`count`**`(`*sub*`[, `*start*`[, `*end*`]])`
Return the number of non-overlapping occurrences of substring *sub* in the range [*start*, *end*]. Optional arguments *start* interpreted as in slice notation.

As you can see, you can learn about various methods you can call on strings such as *capitalize* which is supposed to return a copy of the string with the first character capitalized and the rest lowercased. There is documentation for more than just the Python Language. It exists for almost every decent library, application programming interface, database, web service, or other technical component. Reading documentation is essential to designing and writing your programs. You must know how to interpret the contents of the docs and how it may influence your program design. Sometimes, there are various means of achieving a similar task, and you must decide which method calls or techniques work best for the implementation of your program (an important design decision).

Remember the Reddit program you built earlier? How did I know which URL to use to get the subreddit posts? The documentation has all the answers.

POST **/api/vote** vote   view code #

Cast a vote on a thing.

`id` should be the fullname of the Link or Comment to vote on.

`dir` indicates the direction of the vote. Voting `1` is an upvote, `-1` is a downvote, and `0` is equivalent to "un-voting" by clicking again on a highlighted arrow.

Note: votes must be cast by humans. That is, API clients proxying a human's action one-for-one are OK, but bots deciding how to vote on content or amplifying a human's vote are not. See the reddit rules for more details on what constitutes vote cheating.

`dir`	vote direction. one of (1, 0, -1)
`id`	fullname of a thing
`rank`	an integer greater than 1
`uh / X-Modhash header`	a modhash

If you wanted to extend the functionality of the Reddit program, you could check the docs to see which endpoints are available, the possible request parameters, and the responses. In the previous screenshot, the documentation tells you that the POST method is used to cast a vote and accepts the following parameters: an *id* (the fullname of the link or comment to vote on) and *dir* (vote direction). To test this API call before coding in Python, you could use a program such as Postman to send the POST request with the required authentication and parameters. Then, you could view the response to improve your understanding of how the endpoint works and the response format.

It's important to read the documentation for the packages you install to fully utilize the library. When using a library or tool for GitHub, many of them contain useful documentation or a link to docs in the README file. Remember the *requests* library previously used for HTTP calls in the Reddit program? Well, that is a popular library with detailed documentation. It even contains a quick start guide to get you rapidly up and running. It also outlines advanced usage topics such as web hooks and proxies.

Star 23,625

Requests is an elegant and simple HTTP library for Python, built for human beings. You are currently looking at the documentation of the development release.

Stay Informed

Receive updates on new releases and upcoming projects.

Join Mailing List.

Quickstart

Eager to get started? This page gives a good introduction in how to get started with Request

First, make sure that:

- Requests is installed
- Requests is up-to-date

Let's get started with some simple examples.

Make a Request

Making a request with Requests is very simple.

Begin by importing the Requests module:

```
>>> import requests
```

Now, let's try to get a webpage. For this example, let's get GitHub's public timeline:

```
>>> r = requests.get('https://api.github.com/events')
```

Conclusion

If you want to build advanced applications, you are inevitably going to need to utilize Git, documentation, and a more advanced IDE such as PyCharm. Yet even for the simplest projects, don't underutilize these resources. They will enable you to adopt robust development practices. Amazon Web Services, Docker, Microsoft Azure - these services offer documentation. It's essential you become comfortable and confident reading documentation to successfully develop software. I highly encourage you to explore more of the functionality of Git and the more advanced features of PyCharm.

Final Thoughts

This introduction to Python programming is just a small step in the process of developing your computer science skills and technological literacy. According to College Board, approximately 48,000 students participated in the AP Computer Science A exam in May of 2016, whereas upwards of 450,000 students took the AP United States History Exam. The US education system is lagging behind the technological disruption of this emerging Augmented Age, but it is inevitably changing our culture and economy as we know it. One day at school, I attended a talk at lunch presented by Ian Rowden, a marketing executive who had previously held positions at companies such as Virgin airlines, Coca-Cola, and Callaway. As a successful executive speaking about his experiences in the business world, there was something he said that truly stuck with me. He explained that back in the 1980s and 1990s before technology was as predominant as it currently is, technology was existent to help business. Today, technology is business. Most every growing company is to some degree a technology company.

In the book <u>The New Technology Elite</u>, the author Vinnie Mirchandani describes UPS as a hybrid between a transportation company and a technology company since they have an advanced tracking system and petabytes of data. Nike, once a traditional shoe manufacturer, is fundamentally a tech company. They pioneered wearables with their FuelBand fitness tracker. Not to mention, the company is multifaceted with their retail sales, online sales channel, mobile applications, and social media. The core of Nike's operations, along with most other adapting companies, is powered by software. Traditional businesses and retailers inevitably must adopt technological innovation to remain competitive, profitable, and popular in this business revolution.

The disruption has just begun. The advancement of artificial intelligence (AI), automation, and computing is going to profoundly impact the job market and displace blue collar workers from traditional manufacturing jobs. Billionaire Mark Cuban thinks that AI will displace large numbers of manufacturing jobs in the next three years. Elon Musk, weary of the social effects of AI, thinks that there will be a diminishing number of jobs that robots cannot do better than humans, claiming this is an inevitable even though he doesn't wish for it to happen. In the near future, the labels on our goods will maybe say something along the lines of "Made in America by robots." You must adapt to the ever-changing global nature of our economy. In the Augmented Age, computers will recognize patterns in massive amounts of data, optimize processes, make decisions, and they will be embedded in more objects. Not understanding basic computer science in this day of age is like not knowing about history or mathematics.

Persist through the challenges and at least develop some fundamental understanding of computer science. Law, medicine, retail, manufacturing – all these sectors are becoming fused with technology. Even if you don't want to be an engineer, technology will be a predominant component of your career. Even if you want to be a doctor or politician or litigator or police officer or an executive, you cannot remain competitive and ignore the power of technology. This power will profoundly impact employment and society, with humans no longer acting as the sole decision makers. There are spheres of influence better fit for computers, and others that should remain entirely human. This book was not the be-all-end-all of your computer science education. This was a layer of the foundation and a set of tools. You weren't given fish; you were taught the basics of how to fish and provided with some line and a hook. Go explore, go try new spots, go fish – in deep waters and shallow lagoons. Try building a new Python program, try learning a new programming language, try building a mobile app – do anything besides nothing. You are familiar with basic programming concepts and software development tools. What is incredible about coding is that from anywhere in the world, you have the power to create a software product that can potentially be used by millions of users with little to no startup cost. That is empowerment, with no age barrier or geographical limit.

If you find the process disengaging, think of a higher motive as to why you want to learn computer science. Maybe you want to launch the website you've always dreamed of creating. Maybe you want to build the robot you have always yearned for. If you are like me, maybe you are entrepreneurial and will realize that technology is a remarkable outlet for your pursuits. Much of the process of learning to programming consists of practice and self-led exploration. You will improve your understanding of code through writing code. Set a computer science education goal based off the content of this book, and set out to achieve it through your own research and effort. When I started programming, these drag-and-drop programs and sites such as code.org weren't as prominent as they are today. While these can be helpful resources, I am thankful I started coding before their prevalence. The experience of learning to program without these tools pushed me to read documentation, red programming textbooks, watch college lectures, and truly immerse myself in the topic to pursue my curiosity.

Index

References

"A.1 History of the Software." *A.1 History of the Software*. Python Software Foundation, n.d. Web. 25 Jan. 2017.

"Amazon Prime Air." *Robot Check*. Amazon, n.d. Web. 23 Feb. 2017.

"Automation and Anxiety." *The Economist*. The Economist Newspaper, 25 June 2016. Web. 22 Mar. 2017.

Frey, Carl Benedikt, and Michael A. Osborne. "The Future of Employment: How Susceptible Are Jobs to Computerisation?" *Technological Forecasting and Social Change* 114 (2017): 254-80. Web. 16 Jan. 2017.

Golgowski, Nina. "UPS Is Testing Drone Deliveries, And It's Just As Cool As You'd Hope." *The Huffington Post*. TheHuffingtonPost.com, 22 Feb. 2017. Web. 27 Feb. 2017.

Kuphaldt, Tony R. "Chapter 7 - Boolean Algebra." *Lessons in Electric Circuits*. Vol. IV. N.p.: n.p., 2001. N. pag. Print.

McCandless, David. "Million Lines of Code — Information Is Beautiful." *Information Is Beautiful*. Information Is Beautiful, 24 Sept. 2015. Web. 20 Feb. 2017.

Trikha, Ritika. "The History of 'Hello, World'." *HackerRank Blog*. HackerRank, 07 Mar. 2016. Web. 9 Mar. 2017.

"A Warning from Bill Gates, Elon Musk, and Stephen Hawking." *FreeCodeCamp*. FreeCodeCamp, 19 Feb. 2017. Web. 9 Jan. 2017.

Weisbaum, Herb. "Smart TVs an 'Inevitable' Path for Hackers to Attack Home PCs: Experts." *NBCNews.com*. NBCUniversal News Group, 19 Jan. 2016. Web. 22 Mar. 2017.

www.ingramcontent.com/pod-product-compliance
Lightning Source LLC
Chambersburg PA
CBHW070945050326
40689CB00014B/3352

* 9 7 8 1 5 4 4 1 5 0 2 2 2 *